14214001

INTERDEPENDENCIES OF AGRICULTURE AND RURAL COMMUNITIES

GARLAND REFERENCE LIBRARY
OF SOCIAL SCIENCE
(Vol. 383)

INTERDEPENDENCIES OF AGRICULTURE AND RURAL COMMUNITIES
An Annotated Bibliography

F. Larry Leistritz
Brenda L. Ekstrom

GARLAND PUBLISHING, INC. · NEW YORK & LONDON
1986

Library of Congress Cataloging-in-Publication Data

Leistritz, F. Larry.
Interdependencies of agriculture and rural
communities.

(Garland reference library of social
science ; vol. 383)
Includes indexes.
1. Agriculture—Economic aspects—Bibliography.
2. Agriculture—Social aspects—Bibliography.
3. Rural development—Bibliography.   4. Rural
conditions—Bibliography.   5. Community
development—Bibliography.   I. Ekstrom, Brenda L.
II. Title.   III. Series: Garland reference library
of social science ; v. 383.
Z5074.E3L44   1986   [HD1415]   016.3381   86-22819
ISBN 0-8240-8499-3 (alk. paper)

Printed on acid-free, 250-year-life paper
Manufactured in the United States of America

Dedicated to...

Kenneth E. and Elsie M. Leistritz
Nicolas V. and Sigred H. Engel

Contents

Acknowledgments

Once again, it is our privilege as authors to acknowledge the skills and efficiency of our typist, Lori Cullen. We put her first, for without her assistance, we might not have been able to publish a bibliography on such a current topic in such a short time. She devised ways to effectively manage nearly 600 annotations and thousands of key words to save us a vast amount of time in the book production process. Her contribution is greatly appreciated.

We extend our appreciation to the North Central Regional Center for Rural Development at Ames, Iowa, for providing funds in support of our efforts, which should benefit researchers in the agriculturally dependent North Central region, and to Dr. Peter F. Korsching, Director of the center, for his continued support and encouragement.

We would also like to acknowledge the assistance of the staff of the Interlibrary Loan system at North Dakota State University. Their efforts to promptly secure hundreds of items for us also contributed greatly to the timely production of this book.

In addition, we acknowledge the support of the Department of Agricultural Economics at North Dakota State University and the many researchers who responded to our request for suggestions of books, articles, and reports for inclusion in this bibliography. We wish to especially thank the following persons: Steve H. Murdock and Patricia Bramwell of Texas A&M University; Fred Hines, Tom Carlin, Mary Ahearn, Sara Mazie, and Priscilla Salant of the USDA, Economic Research Service; Rex Campbell of the University of Missouri-Columbia; Ken Stone and Dan Otto of Iowa State University; Ron Wimberley and Robert Morley of North Carolina State University; Roy Rickson of Griffith University, Brisbane, Australia; Peggy Barlett of Emory University; and Glenn Fuguitt of the University of Wisconsin.

As always, our gratefulness to these individuals and entities does not implicate them for any remaining errors or omissions.

Introduction

A variety of economic, social, and political transformations are occurring in rural America. The severe economic problems of the farm sector, the declining relative importance of family-sized commercial farms, the continuing decline in the rural farm population, the decreasing importance of agriculture in the economic base of many rural areas, the increasing dependence of many farm families on off-farm employment as their principal means of livelihood, and the continuing decline of many rural trade centers are only a few of these transformations. For rural communities to adapt to the effects of these changes and stimulate economic growth will require knowledge of the nature of the changes and their impacts on both farm and nonfarm sectors of rural communities. The increasing recognition of the changing nature of rural communities, and particularly the changing patterns of interdependence between farm and nonfarm sectors, has been the basis for a growing research and public policy emphasis in recent years.

The level of resources devoted to these issues has been increasing, but progress is hampered by the difficulty inherent in identifying and accessing relevant works in the area. This difficulty stems in large measure from the multidisciplinary nature of the subject, which results in articles appearing in a wide variety of journals and report series. An additional problem for those seeking an understanding of the changing relationships between agriculture and rural communities is that, although much of the literature is found in readily available professional journals or commercially published texts, many of the most relevant works in the field consist of special reports prepared by agricultural experiment station or extension service personnel, proceedings of conferences, or papers presented at such conferences. Such documents can be very difficult to identify. Thus, scholars and policymakers alike could benefit from a single-source reference work which would help them readily identify key works which relate directly to specific issues (for example, the influence of agricultural structure on community socioeconomic change; off-farm employment of farm household members).

The purpose of this book is to bring together the salient works on socioeconomic change in rural communities, the role of shifts in agricultural structure and technology in stimulating such changes, and conversely, the role of the local economy in influencing farm organization and the lifestyles of farm families. The literature represented reviews the economic, demographic, public service, fiscal, and social changes in rural communities over the past several decades, examines the influence of agricultural structure and technology on community socioeconomic change, investigates the increasing propensity of farm households to engage in off-farm employment, and describes the effects of the current economic stress in agriculture on farm families, agribusiness, and rural communities. The book is an attempt to meet the needs of (1) students of community development, rural sociology, regional and agricultural economics, and related disciplines; (2) teachers and researchers in the academic community; and (3) government agency personnel and policy-makers in both private and public sectors. The specific elements of its focus and scope are discussed below.

Scope

As stated earlier, the focus of this book is on the relationship between agriculture and rural communities. Although research on this relationship has been conducted in many countries, a high percentage of the literature comes from industrialized countries. Therefore, the compilers have concentrated on North American, European, and Australian literature written in English.

Even though the current financial crisis in agriculture has focused attention on agriculture-community interdependencies, literature on the topic is not confined to the 1980s and the current problems in the farm sector; much socioeconomic literature dates back to the early 1900s. For purposes of this bibliography the compilers have concentrated their literature review on the period 1975-1986 although salient works written prior to 1975 were reviewed if they were of enduring interest or formed the basis of later research.

As the book was taking shape, several major topics became apparent: the structure of agriculture and communities, rural development, off-farm employment, part-time farming, financial conditions in agriculture, population shifts between urban and rural areas, rural labor markets, land use, technology, and the role of farm women. These topics encompass most of the works cited in this bibliography.

Methodology

A thorough search of socioeconomic, agricultural, and governmental indexes and of pertinent professional journals yielded a rich body of literature that was considered for inclusion in this book. In addition, a computer bibliographic search was conducted, and suggestions were solicited from leading researchers. Criteria for inclusion of works included methodological or empirical contribution, timeliness, and availability.

Because research in this area has taken on a renewed impetus, much of the literature on the topic has not yet made its way into books but exists as journal articles, governmental reports, and research reports issued by private and public institutions. The compilers were careful to ensure that works selected for this bibliography would be available through libraries or universities or by writing directly to specific agencies. A small body of material also exists as unpublished papers presented at conferences and as dissertations and theses. These works were included only if they were available to the general public and contained useful material not available elsewhere. Addresses of senior authors are given to aid the researcher in acquiring these materials.

Organization of the Bibliography

The bibliography proper is organized by type of publication: (1) books and book chapters, (2) periodicals, (3) federal publications, (4) other research reports, and (5) unpublished papers and dissertations. *Other research reports* includes works published by colleges, universities, and other public or private agencies or research centers. Categorizing proceedings of professional organizations posed a special problem. Proceedings, published in book form, of conferences held once or infrequently were placed in the book category. Proceedings of special conferences sponsored by private or public entities appear in the category with other research reports, and those sponsored annually by professional organizations appear in the periodical section.

Much care was taken to provide the reader with a well-indexed book. The author index includes all authors and/or editors, and the subject index includes up to ten key words for each annotation. The subject index was difficult to construct because of the seemingly endless opportunity to cross reference topics. Many cross references are provided, however, to help the reader wade through the abundance of similar topics. For example, off-farm employment and part-time farming are closely related, but not identical topics. Likewise, the reader will find works indexed under *farm* topics as well as under *structure, agriculture*. Because each annotation concerns agriculture and communities, these two words rarely appear in the index. Theoretically, the entire subject index could be subsumed under these two words. The reader is therefore instructed to think more specifically when using the index. The reader should be further informed that the indexes use citation numbers and not page numbers when referring to location.

Findings

The findings from the literature review reflect the recent history and current status of research concerning the changing patterns of interdependence between the farm and nonfarm sectors of the rural economy. Several major themes are evident in the recent literature. These include (1) effects of changes in the structure of agricultural production on agribusinesses, local trade and service firms, and the social structure of rural communities; (2) recent and prospective changes in the structure of agriculture, with emphasis on the likely influence of new technology and economic stress on the organization and control of agricultural resources; (3) the relative importance of agriculture in the economic base of rural areas; (4) competition for scarce resources between agriculture and other components of the rural economy, with emphasis on land use changes on the urban fringe, competing demands for water in arid regions, and competition for labor resources between agriculture and other rural industries; and (5) the importance of off-farm employment and income for farm families.

Perhaps the most important finding is that one should not overgeneralize about "agriculture" or "rural communities." National averages often conceal great disparities in agricultural structure, the relative importance of agriculture to the rural economy, resource use conflicts, and the prevalance of off-farm employment, both among regions and

among farm types (i.e., farm size and commodity produced).
Nevertheless, certain generalizations can be drawn from
recent literature. These findings are summarized in the
paragraphs which follow.

The influence of agricultural structure on the local
economy and social structure has become the subject of
substantial debate in recent years. Early work in California
appeared to indicate that areas dominated by large farms were
characterized by fewer local business firms, lower levels of
trade and service activity, and a two-tiered social
structure, consisting of farm owner-managers on the one hand
and farm hands on the other. One reason cited for the
negative effect of large-scale farms on community viability
was the tendency for families operating large farms to be
oriented to more distant and larger urban trade centers than
was the case for families who operated smaller farms. More
recent work in other regions of the United States, however,
has cast some doubt on the generality of this relationship.
In particular, recent studies in the Corn Belt and Great
Plains have revealed very little apparent association between
farm size and trade patterns of the operators.

Recent examinations of trends in agricultural structure reveal both considerable differences in the current
patterns of resource ownership and control and substantial
similarities with respect to expected future changes in such
patterns. In general, selected types of crop and livestock
production (especially fruits, vegetables, and cattle
feeding) tend to be dominated by large-scale, industrial-type
farms. Such farms also tend to be concentrated in specific
production regions and particularly in Florida, Texas, and
selected irrigated areas of Arizona and California. Other
regions, such as the western Corn Belt and Great Plains, tend
to be dominated by commercial-scale family farms wherein the
farm operator and family provide the majority of the labor
and depend on farm sales for a majority of their income. In
still other regions part-time farming has become a major, and
sometimes dominant, mode of farm operation.

Although the current structure of agricultural production differs substantially among regions, many observers
believe that the nature of future changes in agricultural
structure will be similar in many areas of the United States.
Both technological advances and adverse economic conditions
are seen to favor development of a bimodal distribution of
farm sizes, with very large farms and small part-time operations gaining at the expense of the family-sized commercial
farm.

Agriculture has traditionally been viewed as a key
component of the economic base of rural areas. In recent

years, however, agriculture has become relatively less significant to the overall economic health of many rural areas.
Growth in manufacturing, government employment, service
industries, and/or retirement communities (sustained in part
by transfer payments) has relegated agriculture to a relatively minor role in the economic bases of many rural areas.
At the same time, in other rural areas agriculture remains a
major, and often the dominant, component of the economic
base. Many areas in the western Corn Belt and Great Plains
fall into this category.

Growing nonagricultural demands for rural resources
often lead to resource use conflicts. Conversion of agricultural land to nonfarm uses is the most widespread example of
such competition. Although nonagricultural users can
generally outbid farmers, some areas have adopted land-use
plans and preferential taxation measures in an attempt to
ensure that the changes in use are orderly and that certain
values associated with agricultural land use (such as green-
space) are preserved.

Finally, perhaps nowhere are the changing patterns of
interdependency between agriculture and rural communities
better illustrated than in the increasing dependence of many
farm families on off-farm employment and income. Nationwide,
nonfarm income now accounts for about 60 percent of the total
income of farm families. Considerable disparities, however,
can be noted among regions and farm size groups; nonfarm
earnings are the most significant for smaller farms
(especially those with total sales less than $40,000) and in
areas with ready access to nonfarm jobs. For increasing
numbers of farm families, then, nonfarm income has apparently
become the key to maintaining their farming operation and
rural lifestyle.

In closing, works annotated in this bibliography
attest to the changing interdependencies of agriculture and
rural communities and illustrate that there are indeed wide
differences in both the nature and degree of those relationships. Formulating appropriate policy responses to these
changing conditions will require an in-depth understanding of
these relationships because the agricultural sector and rural
communities are increasingly sensitive to economic trends and
policies set at state, national, and even international
levels. It is imperative that policymakers be aware of the
far-reaching implications of their actions that may, in
reality, stimulate further changes in these patterns of
interdependency. Evidence of increased interest in these
issues by academicians and policymakers offers hope that farm
and rural development policies will be formulated in an
enlightened atmosphere.

Books
and Book Chapters

Books
and Book Chapters

1. Adams, Bert N. "The Small Trade Center: Processes and Perceptions of Growth or Decline." *The Community: A Comparative Perspective.* Edited by Robert Mills French. Itasca, Illinois: F. E. Peacock Publishers, 1969. pp. 471-84.

   Examines the internal conditions contributing to individual or community stability, to the stages in the loss of services in a declining village, and to people's perceptions of small town economic conditions. Six farm trade centers, two in Missouri and four in Wisconsin, were selected for investigation.

2. Ball, A. Gordon, and Earl O. Heady, eds. *Size, Structure, and Future of Farms.* Ames, Iowa: Iowa State University Press, 1972. 400 pp.

   Attempts to answer some basic social and economic questions relating to the number, size, and structure of farms, and poses some public policy means and alternatives. Topics include economies of size and scale, markets, credit, farm labor, tenure, family and nonfamily corporations, farm groups, and community services.

3. Beale, Calvin L. "The Changing Nature of Rural Employment." *New Directions in Urban-Rural Migration* (item 20), pp. 37-49.

   Examines the diverse and decreasingly agricultural structure of nonmetropolitan employment. Beale studies the change in the dependence on farming (off-farm work and labor force participation by women), employment mix (regional differences; large-scale manufacturing; and mining, service, and public administration), and commuting to metropolitan jobs.

4. Beale, Calvin L. "The Population Turnaround in Rural and Small-Town America." *Rural Policy Problems: Changing Dimensions* (item 21), pp. 47-60.

3

Updates and reevaluates the rural turnaround, noting
the amount and location of the trend, the circumstances
under which it has occurred, the characteristics of the
migrants, and some implications of this major redirection
in the course of U.S. demographic history.

5. Beale, Calvin L. "Quantitative Dimensions of Decline and
   Stability Among Rural Communities." *Communities Left
   Behind: Alternatives for Development* (item 108), pp.
   3-21.

   Summarizes trends of population growth and decline for
   rural towns and counties in the North Central Region over
   the period 1940 to 1970. Implications of these trends
   are discussed.

6. Bellamy, Margot A., and Bruce L. Greenshields, eds. *The
   Rural Challenge*. Contributed papers read at the 17th
   International Conference of Agricultural Economists.
   Aldershot, Hampshire, England: Gower Publishing, 1981.
   329 pp.

   Contains forty papers and forty abstracts of papers
   presented at the 17th International Conference of Agricultural Economists held in 1979. Papers encompass
   topics on the micro, subnational, national, suprana-
   tional, multinational, and diciplinary levels. Also
   included are remarks and discussions on each paper.

   Contains item 14.

7. Bender, Lloyd D. "The Effect of Trends in Economic
   Structures on Population Change in Rural Areas." *New
   Directions in Urban-Rural Migration* (item 20), pp. 137-
   88.

   Considers the effects of changes in rural economic
   structure on population change. Bender's thesis is that
   the structural changes that have been occurring for years
   in rural economies are among the fundamental determinants
   of the population patterns observed now and in the past.

8. Bennett, John W. *Of Time and the Enterprise*.
   Minneapolis: University of Minnesota Press, 1982. 493
   pp.

   Examines agricultural activities in southwestern
   Saskatchewan during the 1960s and early 1970s. The study

was made by anthropologists specializing in social, economic, and ecological analyses. Discussed are agricultural management (defined here as the conduct of agricultural activity), coping with physical resources, the agrifamily system, and management style.

9. Benson, Richard C. "Part-time Farming in a Physically Marginal Area of Northern Ontario." *Part-time Farming: Problem or Resource in Rural Development* (item 51), pp. 114-25.

Examines the incidence of part-time farming in the physically marginal area of the Rainy River District in northern Ontario. Benson concludes that part-time farming in the area has been a long-term persistent situation which has evolved as a symbiotic relationship between agriculture and forestry. The physically marginal conditions have prevented a majority of farmers from establishing viable commercial operations and have forced farmers to seek off-farm employment.

10. Berardi, Gigi M. "Socioeconomic Consequences of Agricultural Mechanization in the United States: Needed Redirections for Mechanization Research." *The Social Consequences and Challenges of New Agricultural Technologies* (item 11), pp. 9-22.

Finds not only a paucity of empirical studies on socioeconomic consequences of mechanization but, among published studies, a high percentage of *ex post facto* research designs. Rarely have the direction and rate of the mechanization process been questioned. Berardi believes that future research should include *ex ante facto* research designs, guard against prevalent "social Darwinist" orientations, and address technology policy issues. Furthermore, compensation and agricultural adjustment programs need to be formulated and evaluated, especially with respect to the actual ability of the rural populations to adjust to new vocations and social environments.

11. Berardi, Gigi M., and Charles C. Geisler, eds. *The Social Consequences and Challenges of New Agricultural Technologies*. Boulder, Colorado: Westview Press, 1984. 376 pp.

Brings together historically relevant research and a
cross section of contemporary studies on the socioeconomic effects of changing agricultural technologies.
Papers from the 1940s and 1950s examine the mechanization of agriculture in the South, in the Midwest, and in
rural areas in general. Other chapters offer present-
day insights on such topics as the socioeconomic consequences of automated vegetable and tobacco harvesting,
center-pivot irrigation, and organic and no-till
cultivation. The authors also discuss compensation and
adjustment programs for displaced labor, the relationship between technology and agribusiness growth, and the
effectiveness of university programs that prepare
students to perform social impact assessments in
agriculture.

Contains items 10, 48, 56, 65, 74.

12. Bescher-Donnelly, Linda, and Leslie Whitener Smith.
    "The Changing Roles and Status of Rural Women." *The
    Family in Rural Society* (item 33), pp. 27-37.

    Examines the increasing role diversity of rural women
    and focuses on their role behavior, functions, and
    responsibilities with respect to four major societal
    institutions: the family, the economy, the educational
    system, and the political structure. Use of this struc-
    tural approach allows recognition of the importance of
    women's roles outside of the family and also draws
    attention to the continued existence of restrictive
    conditions and limited opportunities for many rural
    women.

13. Bible, Alan. "Impact of Corporation Farming on Small
    Business." *Changes in Rural America: Causes, Conse-
    quences, and Alternatives* (item 94), pp. 205-16.

    Summarizes reported effects of corporation farming on
    small business in rural communities, the impact on the
    sociological and moral environment of existing indepen-
    dent family farms and ranches, and likely patterns of
    use of water and other natural resources by corporate
    farm operators.

14. Bollman, Ray D. "Changes at the Urban-Rural Interface:
    The Contribution of Off-farm Work by Farmers." *The
    Rural Challenge* (item 6), pp. 57-64.

Investigates the interrelationships between off-farm work and entry to and exit from farming. Data are drawn from a longitudinal micro data file on Canadian farmers from the 1966, 1971, and 1976 Censuses of Agriculture.

15. Bowers, J. K., and Paul Cheshire. *Agriculture, the Countryside, and Land Use: An Economic Critique.* London: Methuen, 1983. 170 pp.

Attempts to show (1) that British agriculture is undergoing a transformation as momentous as at any time in its history, (2) that this transformation is destroying the British countryside, and (3) that these happenings are brought about neither by technical progress, by population pressure, nor even by urbanization, but rather by misguided policies and excessive support measures. Developments of special concern include the creation of an exalted class of landowning farmers, the elimination of small farmers and agricultural workers, the buildup of agricultural surpluses, the bankruptcy of the CAP (the EEC agricultural policy), the opportunity costs of agricultural support funds, and the steady retraction of the Britisher's time-honored right of access to the countryside.

16. Bradshaw, Ted K., and Edward J. Blakely. "The Changing Nature of Rural America." *Rural Policy Problems: Changing Dimensions* (item 21), pp. 3-18.

Reviews what is being learned about the source of recent rural growth, identifies problems emerging from this growth, and points to some policy directions for effective rural development.

17. Bremer, R. G. *Agricultural Change in an Urban Age: The Loup Country of Nebraska, 1910-1970.* University of Nebraska Studies No. 51. Lincoln, Nebraska: University of Nebraska, 1976. 239 pp.

Focuses on a 900 square mile area of Nebraska to provide insights into the process of agricultural change in a rural community. The book provides an account of (1) agriculture and social conditions up to the beginning of the Depression, (2) subsequent changes following the Depression and the demands of World War II, and (3) the evolution in farm technology. A sociological view of migration, consequences of rural depopulation, and changes in rural education is presented.

18. Brewster, David E., Wayne D. Rasmussen, and Garth
     Youngberg, eds. *Farms in Transition: Interdisciplin-
     ary Perspectives on Farm Structure.* Ames, Iowa: Iowa
     State University Press, 1983. 169 pp.

     Draws together papers by economists, writers, admini-
     strators, political scientists, sociologists, and
     historians that were presented at the symposium on farm
     structure and rural policy held at Iowa State University
     in 1980. Issues discussed include economic policies and
     variables, interest groups, trade, social class, rural
     development, and soil and water conservation.

     Contains items 26, 59.

19. Brown, David L. "A Quarter Century of Trends and
     Changes in the Demographic Structure of American
     Families." *The Family in Rural Society* (item 33), pp.
     9-25.

     Reviews trends and changes in particular dimensions of
     family structure and process as they are described by
     sociodemographic data. Family structure in urban and
     rural areas is compared and contrasted to determine the
     degree to which these trends and changes have permeated
     communities throughout U.S. society.

20. Brown, David L., and John M. Wardwell, eds. *New Direc-
     tions in Urban-Rural Migration.* New York: Academic
     Press, 1980. 412 pp.

     Describes and characterizes the urban-rural migration
     during the 1970s; explores explanations and examines
     consequences of this turnaround; and reviews the poten-
     tials and pitfalls in the use of data resources for
     population distribution research.

     Contains items 3, 7, 34.

21. Browne, William P., and Don F. Hadwiger, eds. *Rural
     Policy Problems: Changing Dimensions.* Lexington,
     Massachusetts: Lexington Books, 1982. 251 pp.

     Contains fifteen chapters presented in four main
     sections: general rural problems, specific rural
     problems, problems of rural local governments, and rural
     policy. This interdisciplinary book combines the work

of sociologists, demographers, economists, political scientists and theorists, and public administrators. Contains items 4, 16, 27, 44.

22. Brunner, Edmund deS. *Rural Trends in Depression Years: A Survey of Village-Centered Agricultural Communities, 1930-1936*. New York: Columbia University Press, 1937. 387 pp.

Presents the results of a study of changes in rural social life in the United States between 1930 and 1936 and traces the life story of 140 village-centered agricultural communities. Brunner analyzes changes in population, in communities, and in the relations of village to country. This book is the third in a series of studies on the same 140 communities.

See also items 23, 24, 341.

23. Brunner, Edmund deS., Gwendolyn S. Hughes, and Marjorie Patten. *American Agricultural Villages*. New York: George H. Doran Company, 1927. 326 pp.

Assembles and interprets field work data about 140 agricultural villages in the United States. An *agricultural village* is defined as a place that has a population between 250 and 2,500 and that is located in a strictly farming area and acts as a service station to the surrounding countryside. Interrelationships between the countryside and village are explored, and detailed data about the economic, social, and religious life of villages are presented.

See also items 22, 24, 341.

24. Brunner, Edmund deS., and J. H. Kolb. *Rural Social Trends*. New York: McGraw-Hill Book Company, 1933. 386 pp.

Studies the factors which underlie and condition rural social life, factors such as (1) the rural population, its mobility, and its changing characteristics; (2) the changing agricultural situation and its social implications; (3) variations in the structure of rural communities; and (4) the interrelationships of country and village dweller and of both with the city. The book concludes with detailed information about the economic,

educational, social, and religious aspects of the life,
organizations, and institutions of rural communities for
the decade 1920-1930. This book builds upon an earlier
study by Brunner on the same 140 agricultural
communities.

See also items 22, 23, 341.

25. Bunce, Michael. "The Contribution of the Part-time
    Farmer to the Rural Economy." *Part-time Farming:
    Problem or Resource in Rural Development* (item 51),
    pp. 249-57.

    Examines the contribution the part-time farmer makes
    to the rural economy as a multiple jobholder and
    explores how this impact is affected by the nature of
    nonfarming occupations. The study, based on a 1973
    survey of farmers in eastern Ontario, identifies five
    parameters which most clearly indicated the variable
    nature of the farmer's off-farm jobholding contribution:
    nonfarm job type, regularity and duration of work,
    employment style, commuting distance, and nonfarm income
    level.

26. Buttel, Frederick H. "Farm Structure and Rural Develop-
    ment." *Farms in Transition: Interdisciplinary
    Perspectives on Farm Structure* (item 18), pp. 103-24.

    Contends that one of the greatest barriers to formu-
    lating innovative policies for the nonmetropolitan
    segment of American society is that the rural farm and
    rural nonfarm components of nonmetropolitan areas are
    considered to be analytically separate and autonomous.
    This view has led to fragmentation among both academi-
    cians and policymakers. As a result, only a small
    degree of attention has been paid to the mutual linkages
    between the development (and underdevelopment) of the
    farm and nonfarm components of nonmetropolitan America.

27. Buttel, Frederick H. "Farm Structure and Rural Develop-
    ment." *Rural Policy Problems: Changing Dimensions*
    (item 21), pp. 213-35.

    Provides an abbreviated overview of available research
    on the interrelations of agricultural and rural develop-
    ment and emphasizes the connections between increasing
    farm size, mechanization, and rural community viability.
    The chapter concludes with (1) a critique of rural

development practice in the United States, particularly in academic and extension circles, and (2) an exploration of prospects for development of agricultural policies that would further the cause of rural development.

28. Clawson, Marion. *Policy Directions For U.S. Agriculture: Long-Range Choices in Farming and Rural Living.* Baltimore: Johns Hopkins Press, 1968. 398 pp.

Takes a comprehensive approach in evaluating effects of alternative agricultural policies. Effects on farm people, farm labor, rural living conditions, migration of farm people, rural institutions and services, rural towns, the spatial organization of agriculture, and its capital structure are considered, in addition to the usual concern with agricultural output, demand, trade, price, and income. A chapter is devoted to the changing role of small towns in rural areas.

29. Clawson, Marion. "Restoration of the Quality of Life in Rural America." *Externalities in the Transformation of Agriculture: Distribution of Benefits and Costs from Development* (item 61), pp. 178-95.

Examines consequences of continued population loss in rural areas. Effects noted include outmigration which is heavily weighted toward younger, better-educated individuals; loss of customers for local businesses; higher per capita costs for services; loss of service quality; and declining asset values in rural towns.

30. Cochrane, Willard W. *The Development of American Agriculture: A Historical Analysis.* Minneapolis: University of Minnesota Press, 1979. 464 pp.

Describes the development of American agriculture and how the development took place in terms of the basic forces that motivated the development process and in terms of the operation of a general conceptual model for the post World War II period. The book is divided into three major parts: a chronological history of American agriculture from 1607 to 1978, an identification of and analysis of key forces involved in development and in structural change, and a conceptual model of agricultural development in the 1950s, 1960s, and 1970s.

31. Cochrane, Willard W., and Mary E. Ryan. *American Farm Policy, 1948-1973.* Minneapolis: University   of Minnesota Press, 1976. 431 pp.

Designed as a reference book that explains and records the U.S. farm policy between 1948 and 1973.   Part I provides a setting for the policy developments, describes the evolution and general content of the programs, and explores the policy formulation process. Part II describes farm policy legislation in detail, and Part III focuses on program mechanics, magnitudes, interrelations, and costs.

32. Coughenour, C. Milton, and Ronald C. Wimberley. "Small and Part-Time Farmers." *Rural Society in the U.S.: Issues for the 1980s* (item 37), pp. 347-56.

Discusses problems of defining small and part-time farmers and identifies the following research needs: gathering descriptive data on small and part-time farm families; identifying localities and   regions where employment and marketing opportunities are limited; identifying the social linkages of new technology with the well-being of farm families; identifying the political socialization and interests of farm families; and understanding the factors and processes of large-scale social and cultural change.

33. Coward, Ray T., and William M. Smith, Jr., eds. *The Family in Rural Society.* Boulder, Colorado: Westview Press, 1981. 238 pp.

Is a collection of readings on the dynamics of family life as it occurs in small towns and rural communities in the United States.   Twelve chapters are organized into four parts: current trends in the family in rural society, patterns and forms of rural families, family dynamics, and prospects and perspectives on rural families.

Contains items 12, 19, 109.

34. Dailey, George H., and Rex R. Campbell. "The Ozark-Ouachita Uplands: Growth and Consequences." *New Directions in Urban-Rural Migration* (item 20), pp. 233-66.

Describes aspects of socioeconomic and demographic change in the Ozarks and delineates some of the important consequences of these changes.

35. Deaton, Brady J. "Relationships of Nonfarm Employment to Agricultural Development." *Interdependencies of Agriculture and Rural Communities in the Twenty-first Century: The North Central Region* (item 514), pp. 171-93.

Organized around the following issues: (1) a historical perspective on structural interrelationships between farm and nonfarm developments; (2) a discussion of the risk orientation of full- and part-time farmers and cumulative growth factors driven by efficiency wages; and (3) strategies for nonfarm employment opportunity growth.

36. Deseran, Forrest A. "Farm and Rural Nonfarm Youth in the Labor Force: Some Observations." *Research in Rural Sociology and Development: Focus on Agriculture* (item 98), pp. 105-33.

Explores labor force participation by rural farm and nonfarm youth. Findings from a national sample of over 3,000 farm and rural nonfarm families with children of labor force age are summarized and assessed.

37. Dillman, Don A., and Daryl J. Hobbs, eds. *Rural Society in the U.S.: Issues for the 1980s*. Boulder, Colorado: Westview Press, 1982. 437 pp.

Contains forty-one articles which examine various forces leading to social and economic changes in rural areas. A group of five chapters deals with the changing structure of agriculture and the effects of those changes on rural communities.

Contains items 32, 57, 62, 93.

38. Edwards, Clark. "The Bases for Regional Growth." *A Survey of Agricultural Economics Literature*. Vol. 3, *Economics of Welfare, Rural Development, and Natural Resources in Agriculture, 1940s to 1970s*. Edited by Lee R. Martin. Minneapolis: University of Minnesota Press, 1981. pp. 159-282.

Reviews the literature in the area and describes five
principles or theories that have been variously
considered in the literature of economics as bases for
growth. An extensive list of references is included.

39. Enyedi, Gyorgy, and Ivan Volgyes, eds. *The Effect of
    Modern Agriculture on Rural Development*. New York:
    Pergamon Press, 1982. 330 pp.

    Contains twenty-three articles which examine the
    effects of agricultural development on rural communities
    in a worldwide context. The contributors address the
    effects of changes in agricultural structure and tech-
    nology on rural development in North America, Europe,
    Israel, Japan, and Puerto Rico. The papers were specif-
    ically commissioned and were delivered at the Fourth
    International Meeting organized by the Commission on
    Rural Development of the International Geographic Union
    in Szeged, Hungary, in 1979.

    Contains items 43, 99.

40. Ewell, Maryo G., Nora E. Fesco, Thomas O. Gamper, Hamed
    M. Ghandorha, Jean R. Jacobus, Jeffrey M. Johnsen,
    Timothy J. Katers, Scot D. Martin, Edward C. Marx, and
    Sandra K. Miller. *A Study of Selected Colorado
    Demographic, Economic, and Social Characteristics with
    Reference to Agricultural and Rural Change*. Denver:
    University of Colorado, Denver, 1985. 75 pp.

    Attempts to provide an understanding of changes and
    current conditions in rural areas and communities of
    Colorado by organizing and analyzing data to determine
    county changes and trends from 1979 through November
    1985.

41. Fassinger, Polly A., and Harry K. Schwarzweller. "The
    Work of Farm Women: A Midwestern Study." *Research in
    Rural Sociology and Development: Focus on Agriculture*
    (item 98), pp. 37–60.

    Explores how and to what extent farm women are
    involved in the organization and work activities of
    contemporary family farms. Data from 124 farm house-
    holds in Michigan were analyzed to determine the
    influence of farm size and family characteristics on the
    work roles of women. Three spheres of work are

considered: housework,   farm   work,   and   off-farm
employment.

42. Field, Donald R., and Robert M. Dimit. "Population
     Change in South Dakota Small Towns and Cities, 1949-
     1960." *Change in Rural America: Causes, Conse-
     quences, and Alternatives* (item 94), pp. 305-11.

     Examines patterns of population change in South Dakota
     communities and comments on some causes and consequences
     of these changes.

43. Fischer, Lewis A.   "The Impact of Modern Agriculture on
     Rural Transformation in Canada."   *The Effect of Modern
     Agriculture on Rural Development* (item 39),   pp. 1-21.

     Identifies some major characteristics of the moderni-
     zation process in Canadian agriculture and assesses
     their impact on rural development.   Government programs
     to foster the economic viability of rural communities
     are reviewed and evaluated.

44. Flinn, William L.   "Communities and Their Relationships
     to Agrarian Values." *Rural Policy Problems: Changing
     Dimensions* (item 21), pp. 19-32.

     Examines rural preferences, farm structure prefer-
     ences, community welfare, public concern, and the conse-
     quences of agricultural structure for rural
     communities.

45. Flora, Cornelia B., and Sue Johnson.   "Discarding the
     Distaff: New Roles for Rural Women."   *Rural U.S.A.:
     Persistence and Change* (item 46), pp. 168-81.

     Examines the role of rural women regarding their
     sexuality, reproduction, socialization of children, and
     production.   The chapter closes with an examination of
     the sources of power and status for rural women and with
     a discussion of rural women's future.

46. Ford, Thomas R.,   ed.   *Rural U.S.A.:   Persistence and
     Change*.   Ames, Iowa: Iowa State University Press,
     1978.   255 pp.

     Contains thirteen original essays dealing with changes
     that are occurring in different segments of rural

society. The authors deal with changes in such areas as
land use, population, technology, values, social organization, public services, the status of minorities, the
role of women, and the incidence of poverty.

Contains item 45.

47. Frauendorfer, Sigmund V. "Part-time Farming: A Review
    of World Literature." Review Article No. 3.   *World.
    Agricultural Economics and Rural Sociology Abstracts*
    Vol. 8, No. 1, 1966. pp. v-xxxviii.

    Reviews and lists 460 international works written
    prior to 1966 on the topic of part-time farming.

48. Friedland, William H.   "A Programmatic Approach to the
    Social Impact Assessment of Agricultural Technology."
    *The Social Consequences and Challenges of New Agricul-
    tural Technologies* (item 11), pp. 197-212.

    Describes combined research and curriculum development
    in social impact assessment (SIA) at the University of
    California, Santa Cruz (UCSC).   The project had two
    concurrent dimensions: (1) research that expands SIA
    methodology to agricultural and technological change;
    and (2) integration of this research into an undergrad-
    uate teaching program.

49. Fuller, Anthony M.   "Part-Time Farming: The Enigmas and
    the Realities." *Research in Rural Sociology and
    Development: Focus on Agriculture* (item 98) pp. 187-
    219.

    Identifies the main attributes of   the part-time
    farming phenomenon and discusses those aspects about
    which there are continuing debates and/or for which the
    prospects for further research are most promising.   An
    extensive review of literature describing part-time
    farming in Europe, Canada, and the   United States
    provides the basis for the author's conclusions.

50. Fuller, Anthony M.   "The Problems of Part-time Farming
    Conceptualised."   *Part-time Farming: Problem or
    Resource in Rural Development* (item 51), pp. 38-56.

    Examines some of the problems derived from Mage's
    conclusion that there are five types of part-time
    farming (item 83):   small-scale hobby, large-scale

hobby, persistent, aspiring, and sporadic. These problems are discussed in terms of their implications particularly in relation to agricultural adjustment and rural development. Examples are drawn from Ontario, Canada.

See also item 83.

51. Fuller, Anthony M., and Julius A. Mage, eds. *Part-time Farming: Problem or Resource in Rural Development.* Proceedings of the First Geography Symposium held at the University of Guelph, Ontario, Canada, 18-20 June 1975. Ontario, Canada: University of Guelph, Department of Geography, 1976. 291 pp.

Presents the proceedings of a conference designed to identify who are the part-time farmers, assess whether part-time farming represents a problem or resource, identify the relationship between newcomers to agriculture and part-time farming, and identify some policy implications.

Contains items 9, 25, 50, 81, 82, 83, 101.

52. Fuller, Varden. "The Consequences of Changes in Agricultural Technology for the Urban Sector and Society as a Whole." *Change in Rural America: Causes, Consequences, and Alternatives* (item 94), pp. 82-88.

Examines the issue of whether rural-reared persons have bettered themselves by moving to the city, and the attributes and influences bearing upon success or failure in achieving assimilation.

53. Geisler, Charles C., and Frank J. Popper, eds. *Land Reform, American Style.* Totowa, New Jersey: Rowman and Allanheld, 1984. 353 pp.

Examines the history of land reform and its relationship with agriculture, natural resources, minorities, rural communities, and urban communities.

Contains item 80.

54. Goldschmidt, Walter. *As You Sow: Three Studies in the Social Consequences of Agribusiness.* Montclair, New Jersey: Allanheld, Osmun and Company, 1947 and 1978. 505 pp.

Documents, through a study of three California towns, the impact of corporate agriculture on the character of life in rural American communities. It is a widely referenced, classic study of rural life. Goldschmidt studies the social and agricultural structure of rural America, the social consequences of corporate farming, and the political power of agribusiness.

Compare with items 76, 223, 238, 243, 490.

55. Gregor, Howard F. *Industrialization of U.S. Agriculture: An Interpretive Atlas.* Boulder, Colorado: Westview Press, 1982. 259 pp.

Offers a geographic view of the industrialization of American agriculture through a study of the intensity, scale, structure, types, and performance of industrialization.

56. Hamilton, C. Horace. "The Social Effects of Recent Trends in the Mechanization of Agriculture." *The Social Consequences and Challenges of New Agricultural Technologies* (item 11), pp. 63-71.

Focuses on mechanization in the Cotton Belt, especially the difficulties which faced displaced tenants, share croppers, and the rising transient labor force. In this reprinted 1939 article the author discusses the dependence of farmers on outside economic forces--monopolistic farm-machinery corporations and large oil companies--which had come to control a large share of agricultural income.

57. Havens, A. Eugene. "The Changing Structure of U.S. Agriculture." *Rural Society in the U.S.: Issues for the 1980s* (item 37), pp. 308-16.

Discusses a variety of research issues concerning the changing structure of U.S. agriculture and poses a model for analyzing these changes. Research needs include (1) analyzing the changes and developing a link between changes in agriculture and the broader political economy and (2) analyzing how the political processes present rural families with changing conditions for survival and how families attempt to respond by presenting the state with contradictory demands for subsidies, cheap credit, restricted land use, new markets, more water, and new technology or for a noninterventionist policy.

58. Hawley, Amos H., and Sara Mills Mazie, eds. *Nonmetropolitan America in Transition*. Chapel Hill, North Carolina: University of North Carolina Press, 1981. 833 pp.

Is a collection of original articles on the economic, demographic, and other changes taking place in rural America. Articles are organized into the following five topics: The Deconcentration of Population; The Changing Structure of Economic Opportunity; The Differential Access to Opportunity; The Distribution of Amenities; and Growth, Environmental Impact, and Planning.

Contains item 77.

59. Heady, Earl O. "Economic Policies and Variables: Potentials and Problems for the Future." *Farms in Transition: Interdisciplinary Perspectives on Farm Structure* (item 18), pp. 23-35.

Examines the effect of U.S. agricultural policies on changes in farm structure and outlines some implications of these changes in structure for rural communities. The author defines *structure* as referring to the size and number of farms, the amount of capital and labor employed per farm and in the industry, the degree of specialization, and related parameters. If farm size increases and numbers decrease substantially, the social and economic environment of agriculturally dependent communities will deteriorate.

60. Heady, Earl O. "Rural Development and Rural Communities of the Future." *Rural Industrialization: Problems and Potentials*. Edited by Larry R. Whiting. Ames, Iowa: Iowa State University Press, 1974. pp. 136-50.

Points out that the crux of the rural development problem is one of inequity in the distribution of gains and costs of technological and economic development of state and national levels. The central task then is to identify the nature, location, and extent of inequities falling on rural communities and various population strata of them, and then to evaluate and provide alternative means of alleviating or redressing them. In favored locations, some of these inequities can be erased through industrialization. In a greater number of locations, however, the inequities can be removed only through entirely different means and programs.

61. Heady, Earl O., and Larry R. Whiting, eds. *Externali-*
     ties in the Transformation of Agriculture: Distribu-
     tion of Benefits and Costs from Development. Ames,
     Iowa: Iowa State University Press, 1975. 341 pp.

     Contains fifteen papers dealing with the distribution
     of benefits and costs of agricultural development.
     Papers represent experiences from Africa, Asia, Europe,
     and Latin America as well as the United States. Govern-
     ment policy to achieve a more equitable distribution of
     costs and benefits is a major interest of several
     authors.

     Contains items 29, 73.

62. Heffernan, William D. "Structure of Agriculture and
     Quality of Life in Rural Communities." *Rural Society*
     in the U.S.: Issues for the 1980s (item 37), pp. 337-
     46.

     Addresses the relationship between agricultural struc-
     ture and quality of life in rural communities.
     Heffernan reviews past literature, then presents the
     following research needs: identify key variables in the
     agricultural system that, if altered, lead to a change
     in the quality of community life; focus on the input,
     marketing, processing, and distribution sectors of the
     agricultural sector; determine whether groups and
     collective-bargaining associations are effective means
     for producers to maintain or increase their power;
     research the relationships that exist among agricultural
     structure, ecology, and quality of life; determine
     whether the social life of rural communities will be
     affected by future changes in the structure of agricul-
     ture; and develop a better understanding of the impact
     of changes in the larger society (including government
     rules and regulations) on the structure of agriculture
     and rural communities.

63. Higbee, Edward. *Farms and Farmers in an Urban Age.* New
     York: The Twentieth Century Fund, 1963. 183 pp.

     Examines the consequences of the extensive mechaniza-
     tion of American agriculture. Past changes in the use
     of capital and labor, value of production, land use, and
     other salient farm characteristics are examined, and
     future changes in the structure of agriculture are
     postulated.

64. Hodge, Ian, and Martin Whitby. *Rural Employment: Trends, Options, Choices.* London: Methuen, 1981. 262 pp.

Maintains that rural labor markets are at the core of the problem of rural depopulation in developed countries and that the success of policies seeking to moderate the process of population decline will be closely related to the policymaker's ability to influence labor markets constructively. The renewal of rural population is not simply a matter of the balance of births over deaths: migration in search of work has been a major cause of rural decline and its reversal, to bring about economically viable communities, must be related to the availability of employment in rural areas. Rural employment trends ard rural development programs in the United Kingdom, Australia, Canada, and the United States are examined.

65. Hussen, Ahmed M. "Assessment of the Economic and Social Impacts of Agricultural Technology: A Case Study." *The Social Consequences and Challenges of New Agricultural Technologies* (item 11), pp. 121-42.

Reviews models and methodologies used for technology assessment, all of which tend to overemphasize economic factors and underemphasize secondary and tertiary impacts of technology. The author argues that many of the models do not take into account all the distributional effects (social and economic) arising from agricultural technology. Hussen uses a framework for analysis similar to Schmitz and Seckler's to estimate gross and net social returns resulting from use of the mechanical strawberry harvester in Oregon.

See also item 383.

66. Iowa State University, Center for Agricultural and Economic Development. *Farm Goals in Conflict: Family Farm, Income, Freedom, Security.* Ames, Iowa: Iowa State University Press, 1963. 251 pp.

Is a collection of papers by major farm and nonfarm groups with programs and activities which necessarily assume certain values and goals for agriculture.

67. Iowa State University, Center for Agricultural and
     Economic Development. *Structural Changes in Commer-*
     cial Agriculture. CAED Rpt. 24. Ames, Iowa: Iowa
     State University, 1965. 262 pp.

     Collects papers presented at a conference on struc-
     tural changes in commercial agriculture and what these
     changes mean for marketing firms, research institutions,
     and educational agencies.

68. Jansma, J. Dean, Hays B. Gamble, J. Patrick Madden, and
     Rex H. Warland. "Rural Development: A Review of
     Conceptual and Empirical Studies." *A Survey of Agri-*
     cultural Economics Literature. Vol. 3, *Economics of*
     Welfare, Rural Development, and Natural Resources in
     Agriculture, 1940s to 1970s. Edited by Lee R. Martin.
     Minneapolis: University of Minnesota Press, 1981.
     pp. 285-361.

     Focuses on reviewing literature which addresses the
     issue of (1) social and economic aspects of rural
     development (with emphasis on income and employment
     considerations), (2) the role of organizational and
     institutional forces in the development process, and (3)
     the impact of alternative spatial arrangements on rural
     development activities.

69. Johansen, Harley E., and Glenn V. Fuguitt. *The Changing*
     Rural Village in America: Demographic and Economic
     Trends Since 1950. Cambridge, Massachusetts:
     Ballinger Publishing Company, 1984. 259 pp.

     Defines villages as places of less than 2,500 popula-
     tion and examines their role in the economic and social
     life of rural America. The authors find that both the
     number and aggregate population of villages nationwide
     increased during the 1970s. In fact, during this period
     the percentage growth in village population exceeded
     that of the nation as a whole.

70. Johnson, Gale, ed. *Food and Agricultural Policy for the*
     1980s. Washington, D.C.: American Enterprise
     Institute for Public Policy Research, 1981. 229 pp.

     Collects selected papers presented at the Conference
     on Food and Agricultural Policy sponsored by the Ameri-
     can Enterprise Institute in 1980. Topics include
     economic developments affecting food and agriculture in

part-time farming on a regional scale and presents the
results of an analysis contributing to terminology and a
better understanding of who part-time farmers are. The
discussion centers around Ontario, Canada.

84. Marshall, Ray. *Rural Workers in Rural Labor Markets.*
    Salt Lake City, Utah: Olympus Publishing Company,
    1974. 183 pp.

    Is the result of a project to determine the manpower
    structure of rural labor markets, past and present.
    Some of the topics discussed include migration and
    income differentials; future of small farmers; migrant
    workers; rural economic development; rural manpower
    programs; rural organizations; and policy recommenda-
    tions to improve the economic conditions of small
    farmers, agricultural workers, and low-income nonfarm
    residents.

85. Marshall, Ray, James L. Walker, and R. Lynn Rittenoure.
    Human Resource Development in Rural Texas. Studies in
    Human Resource Development No. 1. Austin, Texas:
    University of Texas, Center for the Study of Human
    Resources and Bureau of Business Research, 1974. 120
    pp.

    Is divided into three major sections: rural popula-
    tion and employment, implications and impact of rural
    development, and rural manpower programs. More specif-
    ically, topics include population changes, rural labor
    force, education, industrialization potential of
    nonmetropolitan Texas, and effects of commuting
    patterns.

86. Merrill, Richard. "Agribusiness and the Decaying Rural
    Environment." *Change in Rural America: Causes,
    Consequences, and Alternatives* (item 94), pp. 250-55.

    Points out that large agribusiness firms have gained
    considerable control over agricultural production,
    especially in the South and West and particularly in
    Florida, California, Texas, Arizona, and Hawaii.
    Corporate influence is very substantial in such
    specialty crops as citrus fruit, melons, and vegetables
    and in cattle feeding. Implications of the growing
    corporate influence are discussed.

87. Montague, Meg. "Internal Migration and Rural Depopula-
    tion." *Planning in Turbulent Environments*. Edited by
    John S. Western and Paul R. Wilson. St. Lucia,
    Queensland, Australia: University of Queensland
    Press, 1977. pp. 163-82.

    Investigates the sociological features of population
    movement from a rural shire in central western Queens-
    land. A brief overview of the area and its population
    is presented before the description of the ex-residents
    and the discussion of differential factors operating in
    the process by which they became migrants, their motiva-
    tion for migrating, and their eventual destination.

88. Murdock, Steve H., and F. Larry Leistritz. "Effects on
    Agriculture and Local Businesses." *Energy Development
    in the Western United States*. New York: Praeger
    Publishers, 1979. pp. 144-73.

    Examines potential effects of energy development on
    agriculture and on local trade and service firms in
    affected areas.

89. Newby, Howard. *The Deferential Worker: A Study of Farm
    Workers in East Anglia*. Madison, Wisconsin: Univer-
    sity of Wisconsin Press, 1979. 486 pp.

    Examines the agricultural worker in a historical and
    sociological context and discusses the rural labor
    market, agricultural trade unionism, the work situation,
    changes in the rural village, and images of self and
    society. The study focuses on East Anglia, England.

90. Paulsen, Arnold, and Jerry Carlson. "Is Rural Main
    Street Disappearing?" *Change in Rural America:
    Causes, Consequences, and Alternatives* (item 94), pp.
    64-65.

    Points out the effects of farm consolidation on main
    street businesses in rural towns. Consolidation will
    have differential effects on different types of
    businesses. Consumer-goods businesses are most affected
    by changes in net farm income and the number of farmers
    in the area. Production-goods businesses are most
    sensitive to changes in the volume of production and
    hence the level of expenditures for production inputs.
    Finally, firms engaged in handling, transporting, and

processing farm products are most affected by changes in the physical volume of farm output.

91. Price, Barry L. *The Political Economy of Mechanization in U.S. Agriculture.* Boulder, Colorado: Westview Press, 1983. 108 pp.

Contributes to the debate over public funding of agricultural mechanization research, which some contend benefits only restricted segments of the population, particularly large growers. The author raises fundamental questions about economic methods used to calculate social returns on research. A case study of the electronic tomato sorter is conducted to exemplify key issues.

92. Rodefeld, Richard D. "The Nature, Magnitude, and Consequences of Change in Farm Organizational, Occupational, and Class Structure." *Change in Rural America: Causes, Consequences, and Alternatives* (item 94), pp. 121-28.

Provides an overview of questions and issues concerning changes in the organizational structure of agriculture and possible implications of these changes. Central to the discussion are the questions of (1) whether family-operated farms are being replaced by larger corporate or "industrial-type" farms and (2) what the implications of such a change would be.

93. Rodefeld, Richard D. "Who Will Own and Operate America's Farms?" *Rural Society in the U.S.: Issues for the 1980s* (item 37), pp. 328-36.

Presents some current information on who owns, manages, and works U.S. farms and discusses the implications of recent changes. The following research needs are presented: improved monitoring of farm characteristics and their changes in the 1980's; research on the consequences of change for nonfarm sectors of rural and urban United States; and information on the causes of changes in farm ownership, management, and labor.

94. Rodefeld, Richard D., Jan Flora, Donald Voth, Isao Fujimoto, and Jim Converse, eds. *Change in Rural America: Causes, Consequences, and Alternatives.* St. Louis: C. V. Mosby Company, 1978. 551 pp.

Focuses on changes in the rural sector that have occurred in agricultural technology, farm organizational and occupational structure, transportation, communication, urban population distribution, and the rural economic base.

Contains items 13, 42, 52, 86, 90, 92.

95. Rogers, David L., Larry Whiting, and Judy A. Anderson, eds. *An Annotated Bibliography of Rural Development Research in the North Central Region.* Ames, Iowa: North Central Regional Center for Rural Development, 1975. 229 pp.

Summarizes rural development research performed between 1967 and 1974 in the North Central region by scientists affiliated with Agricultural Experiment Stations. Literature cited is classified into eight categories: (1) population composition and movement, (2) employment, income, and wealth, (3) economic services and facilities, (4) social services, (5) natural resources, (6) individual and family decision making, (7) group and community decision making, and (8) general rural development theory. Some references to work that is relevant to each of these areas are included even though the research may have been performed by scientists outside the experiment stations and, in some instances, outside the twelve-state region.

96. Roseman, Curtis C., Andrew J. Sofranko, and James D. Williams, eds. *Population Redistribution in the Midwest.* Ames, Iowa: Iowa State University, North Central Regional Center for Rural Development, 1981. 222 pp.

Discusses the demographic, geographic, historical, and policy aspects of the recent population redistribution patterns. Also discussed is the set of issues which have emerged with this redistribution, issues such as urban migrants to rural areas, industry's role in nonmetropolitan economic development and population change, and local politics.

97. Roussos, Dean S. "A Study of Changes in Retail Sales Patterns by City Size Classes." *Urban Responses to Agricultural Change* (item 75), pp. 141-49.

Examines changes in sales volume of farm production goods from 1948 to 1954 for different size classes of Iowa towns. During this period retail sales increased more rapidly in the smaller towns than in Iowa's cities. The author indicates that a major source of the increased sales volume in communities of less than 2,500 was purchases of farm equipment, lumber, hardware, and feed by farmers.

98. Schwarzweller, Harry K., ed. *Research in Rural Sociology and Development: Focus on Agriculture.* Vol. 1. Greenwich, Connecticut: JAI Press Inc., 1984. 353 pp.

Contains fourteen chapters dealing with various aspects of agricultural structure and rural life. Separate chapters are devoted to part-time farming, the influence of farm structural characteristics on trade patterns, work by farm women, and rural youth in the labor force.

Contains items 36, 41, 49, 76.

99. Scott, Peter. "Agricultural Change and Rural Stability in Australia." *The Effect of Modern Agriculture on Rural Development* (item 39), pp. 65-84.

Focuses on recent changes in farm numbers and the rural population against a background of the changing enterprise structure of Australian farming in response to changing cost-price relationships. It pays particular attention to the intercensal period 1966-1971 when the rural sector underwent the greatest upheaval of any postwar intercensal period.

100. Simon, William, and John H. Gagnon. "The Decline and Fall of the Small Town." *The Community: A Comparative Perspective.* Edited by Robert Mills French. Itasca, Illinois: F. E. Peacock Publishers, 1969. pp. 497-510.

Presents a detailed analysis of three neighboring rural towns in southern Illinois to determine why, despite many similarities in location, economic problems, and history, they developed differently after World War II. The area had been dependent largely on the coal industry, and declining mining activity forced

all three communities to seek means to strengthen and
diversify their economic base.

101. Stock, George. "Off-farm Work by Small Scale Farmers
     in Ontario." *Part-time Farming: Problem or Resource
     in Rural Development* (item 51), pp. 68-82.

     Describes the relationship between small-scale
     farming and off-farm work and examines the characteris-
     tics of off-farm work as it applies to small-scale farm
     operations.

102. Summers, Gene F., ed. *Technology and Social Change in
     Rural Areas: A Festschrift for Eugene A. Wilkening.*
     Boulder, Colorado: Westview Press, 1983. 266 pp.

     Begins with a discussion of the changing paradigms of
     technology adoption and diffusion, the dynamics of
     public resistance, and the question of social responsi-
     bility in an age of synthetic biology. The book then
     goes on to present discussions on the revolutionary
     effect of technology on agriculture worldwide and on
     the transformations of rural life and communities that
     result from localized effects of technology and its use
     as a weapon in world-system politics.

103. Tweeten, Luther. "New Policies to Take Advantage of
     Opportunities for Agricultural and Rural Develop-
     ment." *Interdependencies of Agriculture and Rural
     Communities in the Twenty-first Century: The North
     Central Region* (item 514), pp. 215-26.

     Reviews rural opportunities and problems and suggests
     an appropriate federal response.

104. Tweeten, Luther. "Prospective Changes in U.S. Agricul-
     tural Structure." *Food and Agricultural Policy for
     the 1980s* (item 70), pp. 113-46.

     Attempts to close some of the gaps in the literature
     on the structure of agriculture and then projects
     changes in farming structure. Positive and negative
     elements in the changes are reviewed, and sources of
     growth in farm size are estimated and projected to the
     year 2000.

105. Tweeten, Luther, and George L. Brinkman. *Micropolitan
     Development: Theory and Practice of Greater-Rural*

Economic Development. Ames, Iowa: Iowa State University Press, 1976. 456 pp.

Presents a comprehensive look at greater-rural development and attempts to integrate literature on micropolitan development into a meaningful whole. The definition of micropolitan (or nonmetropolitan) development requires that cities of up to 50,000 population, which serve as centers of trade, services, and jobs, must be included in addition to rural towns when examining rural development.

106. University of Florida. *Agricultural Growth in an Urban Age.* Gainesville, Florida: University of Florida, Institute of Food and Agricultural Sciences, 1975. 230 pp.

Assesses the present and future role of agriculture in Florida, a largely urban state in which agricultural growth often occurs in a political and social setting heavily influenced by urban interests.

107. Vogeler, Ingolf. *The Myth of the Family Farm: Agribusiness Dominance of U.S. Agriculture.* Boulder, Colorado: Westview Press, 1981. 352 pp.

Examines the struggle between land interests in the private and public sectors and finds that the myth of the family farm has been used to obscure the dominance of agribusiness and that corporate penetration of agriculture has in turn contributed to the plight of migrant workers, the decline of small towns, and the economic difficulties of independent farmers. Vogeler identifies major shortcomings of agribusiness and federal land-related laws and programs, examines regional impacts of agribusiness and federal farm programs on rural areas, and considers the role of racial minorities and women in the development of agrarian capitalism.

108. Whiting, Larry R., ed. *Communities Left Behind: Alternatives for Development.* Ames, Iowa: Iowa State University Press, 1974. 151 pp.

Identifies some of the characteristics, entities, and amenities desirable to human life within rural communities. The book covers such topics as quantitative dimensions of decline and stability, social and family adjustment to decline, service structures, enhancing economic and social opportunity, and feasible options for social action and economic development.

Contains item 5.

109. Wilkening, Eugene A. "Farm Families and Family Farming." *The Family in Rural Society* (item 33), pp. 27-37.

Examines (1) what changes in the farm enterprise have occurred in recent decades that have significance for the farm family, (2) how the farm family has become involved in work off the farm as an adaptation to these changing economic forces, (3) the definitions and characteristics of the family farm, (4) the involvement of women in the farm enterprise and changes in attitudes toward men's and women's roles and (5) some suggestions for further research pertaining to the relationship of farm and family.

110. Wimberley, Ronald C. "The Emergence of Part-Time Farming As a Social Form of Agriculture." *Research in Sociology of Work: Peripheral Workers.* Vol. 2. Edited by Ida H. Simpson and Richard L. Simpson. Greenwich, Connecticut: JAI Press, 1983. pp. 325-56.

Reviews recent findings which call attention to part-time farming and some of its implications for further phases of research and theoretical explanation. Wimberley provides descriptive information on part-time farming, who these farmers are, where they are, what they do, some contemporary trends in part-time farming, and some issues involved. In addition, part-time farming is viewed from the wider context of structural changes in American agriculture.

Periodicals

Periodicals

111. Adams, Richard M., and Dale J. Menkhaus. "The Effect of Mining on Agricultural Hired Labor in the Northern Great Plains." *American Journal of Agricultural Economics* 62, No. 4(1980):748-52.

Investigates the nature of the market for hired agricultural labor in the Northern Great Plains with particular reference to adjustments attendant to energy development. Specific objectives include (1) specification of a regional labor market model defining the supply and demand for hired agricultural labor; (2) assessment of the importance of wages in agriculture and mining in explaining the supply of labor to agriculture, with emphasis on the plausibility of mining growth as an incentive for the transfer of labor out of agriculture; and (3) comparision of these results with earlier supply and demand studies for agricultural labor.

112. Ahearn, Mary, Jim Johnson, and Roger Strickland. "The Distribution of Income and Wealth of Farm Operator Households." *American Journal of Agricultural Economics* 67, No. 5(1985):1087-94.

Describes the financial well-being of farm operator households by measuring their size distribution of personal income and farm equity in 1984 and by analyzing the contribution of each source of income to the total inequality of incomes.

113. Aitchison, J. W., and P. Aubrey. "Part-time farming in Wales: A Typological Study." *Institute of British Geographers* (Transactions New Series) 7, No. 1(1982): 88-97.

Identifies types of part-time farming systems in Wales, based on a sample of 211 agricultural holdings and a mixed-mode set of five variables. Six types are

identified, and the motives underlying the   decision to
farm part-time are discussed.

114.   Albrecht, Don, and Howard Ladewig.   "Corporate Agricul-
       ture and the Family Farm."   *The Rural Sociologist* 2,
       No. 6(1982):376-83.

       Compares family and corporate   (nonfamily-held) farms
       in the following terms: number, size, sales, commodi-
       ties produced, and location.   The 1978 Census of Agri-
       culture is the primary data source.

115.   Albrecht, Don E.   "Agricultural Dependence and the
       Population Turnaround: Evidence from the Great
       Plains."   *Journal of the Community Development
       Society* 17, No. 1(1986):1-15.

       Uses data for the   period   1940 to   1980   from   294
       nonmetropolitan Great   Plains counties   to   show   that
       reduced agricultural dependence   is   a   major   factor
       influencing the rural-urban migration turnaround of the
       1970s.   The results   indicate   that   counties heavily
       dependent   on   agricultural employment   were   about   as
       likely to   experience population   declines   during   the
       1970s as they were during earlier decades.   There were
       fewer   such counties,   however, and thus   their overall
       influence   was   reduced.   The   consequences   of   these
       findings for   rural communities   in   major agricultural
       areas are discussed.

116.   Albrecht, Don E., and Steve H. Murdock.   "In Defense of
       Ecological   Analyses of Agricultural   Phenomena: A
       Reply to Swanson and Busch."   *Rural Sociology* 50, No.
       3(1985):438-56.

       Rebuts criticisms by Swanson and Busch of   an earlier
       article   by Albrecht   and Murdock   that   applied   human
       ecological   theory to   explain the prevalence   of part-
       time farming in sections of the United States.

       A rebuttal to item 376 in defense of item 118.

117.   Albrecht, Don E.,   and Steve H. Murdock.   "Natural
       Resource Availability and Social Change."   *Sociologi-
       cal Inquiry* 56, No. 3(1986).   In press.

       Attempts to empirically test the assumptions that the
       natural   resource base   of a   society   establishes   the

limits or constraints within which that society must operate by looking at the effects of groundwater availability in the U.S. Great Plains from 1940 to 1980. A model derived from human ecology theory was used to determine that irrigation development had major implications on nonmetropolitan counties during the time period studied. Irrigation development resulted in increased agricultural production, in variations in the structure of farm enterprises, and in increased retention of both farm and nonfarm populations.

118. Albrecht, Don E., and Steve H. Murdock. "Toward a Human Ecological Perspective on Part-time Farming." *Rural Sociology* 49, No. 3(1984):389-411.

Applies human ecological theory to explain the growing prevalence of part-time farming in various parts of the United States. Variables depicting the farm and nonfarm environmental, technological, and sustenance bases are examined.

Refuted by item 376, which is rebutted by item 116.

119. Albrecht, Don E., and John K. Thomas. "Farm Tenure: A Retest of Conventional Knowledge." *Rural Sociology* 51, No. 1(1986):18-30.

Finds that Texas crop producers who rented most or all of their farmland had the largest and most productive farms, used better farming practices, and were more involved in community affairs. These findings are contrasted with those of fifty years ago, when tenant farmers generally used less effective farming practices, were less involved in community affairs, were younger, and had less education.

120. Ballard, Patricia L., and Glenn V. Fuguitt. "The Changing Small Town Settlement Structure in the United States, 1900-1980." *Rural Sociology* 50, No. 1(1985):99-113.

Examines interdecade growth of U.S. nonmetropolitan incorporated places, grouped by initial size and location, for each decade since 1900. Results show four periods of growth and decline: 1900-1930, continuous rural settlement and overall concentration;

1930-1940, depressed urban growth; 1940-1960, suburban-
ization and rural decline; and 1960-1980, deconcentration and village revival.

121. Barbic, Ana. "The Farmer-Worker in Yugoslavia: A
      Bridge Between the City and the Country." *Sociologia
      Ruralis* 23, No. 1(1983):76-84.

      Examines patterns of part-time farming in Yugoslavia
      not only from the aspect of multiple jobholding but
      also from the dimension of movement between the place
      of residence and place of work.

122. Barkley, Paul W.   "A Contemporary Political Economy of
      Family Farming." *American Journal of Agricultural
      Economics* 58, No. 5(1976):812-19.

      Presents some definitions of the family farm and
      political economy; comments on production, exchange,
      and distribution within agriculture; and discusses
      agriculture's place in the political economy.

123. Barlett, Peggy F. "Microdynamics of Debt, Drought, and
      Default in South Georgia." *American Journal of Agri-
      cultural Economics* 66, No. 5(1984):836-43.

      Reports   results   of   an   in-depth   study   of farm
      operators in Dodge County, Georgia. Severe droughts,
      together with the general economic climate for agricul-
      ture, have led to high rates of loan default in the
      state. The study indicates that large commercial
      farmers and younger renter-farmers face the most
      serious financial problems.

124. Bass, Peter L., and Edward M. Kirshner. "Demographic,
      Economic, and Fiscal Impacts of Alternative Westlands
      Reclamation Act Enforcement Scenarios." *American
      Journal of Agricultural Economics* 60, No.
      5(1978):935-44.

      Summarizes projected demographic, economic, and
      fiscal changes that might occur to the year 1990 under
      different enforcement schemes in the Westlands Water
      District of California. Four levels of enforcement of
      the 1902 Reclamation Act provisions regarding farm
      size, residency, and land price are postulated. The
      community effects of different enforcement levels are
      measured through changes in resident employment,

population, households, retail sales, and costs and revenues for school districts and municipalities.

125. Bateman, W. Lanny, Odell L. Walker, and Raleigh A. Jobes. "On Part-time Farming." *Southern Journal of Agricultural Economics* 6, No. 2(1974):137-42.

Documents the increasing importance of part-time farmers in twelve southern states. A significant amount of the beef production resources in the South are under the control of part-time farmers. Economic logic and preliminary empirical investigations are presented to indicate that part-time farming has potential impacts on organization of beef production, beef supply response, and the rural economic environment.

126. Beale, Calvin L. "The Population Turnaround in Rural and Small Town America." *Policy Studies Review* 2, No. 1(1982):43-54.

Updates and reevaluates the rural population turnaround with data through 1980, noting the amount and location of this trend, the circumstances under which it has occurred, the characteristics of the migrants, and some implications of this redirection of population.

127. Beaulieu, Lionel J., and Joseph J. Molnar. "Community Change and the Farm Sector: Impacts of Rural Development on Agriculture." *The Rural Sociologist* 5, No. 1(1985):15-22.

Examines some of the more critical elements within the local community setting that influence agriculture, namely population, employment, land use, water, and environment.

128. Belongia, Michael T., and R. Alton Gilbert. "The Farm Credit Crisis: Will It Hurt the Whole Economy?" *Review (The Federal Reserve Bank of St. Louis)* 67, No. 10(1985):5-15.

Makes some comparisons and contrasts between the farm financial crisis of the 1920s and the 1980s and discusses the implications for the economy as a whole.

129. Bennett, Claude F.   "Mobility from Full-time to Part-
      time Farming."   *Rural Sociology* 32, No. 2(1967):154-
      64.

      Assesses factors that   may be associated with the
      shift from full-time to part-time farming.   Farm
      income, farm income per family member, proximity to
      numerous nonfarm jobs, and operator age each had a
      statistically significant correlation with the shift to
      part-time farming; educational level did not.   A multi-
      variate analysis showed that none of these predicted
      the shift regardless of the level of magnitude of the
      independent variables.

130. Bertrand, Alvin L.   "Research on   Part-Time Farming in
      the United States."   *Sociologia Ruralis* 7(1967):295-
      306.

      Reviews research up to 1967 dealing with part-time
      farming (i.e., combining farm and off-farm work) in the
      United States.   Topics covered   include (1) definition
      of part-time farms, (2) individual motivation for part-
      time farming, (3) classes and career patterns of part-
      time farmers, (4) the role of part-time farming in
      agricultural adjustment, (5) social organization impli-
      cations of part-time farming, and (6) the future of
      part-time farming.

131. Bird, S. Elizabeth.   "The Impact of Private Estate
      Ownership on Social Development in a Scottish Rural
      Community." *Sociologia Ruralis* 22, No. 1(1982): 43-
      56.

      Examines the effect which decisions made by a private
      landowning family have had on the development of a
      rural community in western Scotland and uses this as a
      case study to demonstrate the widespread and continuing
      impact of landowners' decisions on Scottish rural life
      generally.

132. Blair, A. M.   "Urban Influences on Farming in Essex."
      Geoforum 11 (1980):371-84.

      Presents results of a large-scale farm survey which
      sought to examine the effects of urban proximity on
      farm management practices in Essex County, England.
      The article examines the nature and spatial extent of
      the conversion of farm land to urban uses, changes in

farm labor, part-time farming, vandalism, farm-based recreation, and the sale of produce direct to the public.

133. Bokemeier, Janet L., Carolyn Sachs, and Verna Keith. "Labor Force Participation of Metropolitan, Nonmetropolitan, and Farm Women: A Comparative Study." *Rural Sociology* 48, No. 4(1983):515-39.

Identifies socioeconomic correlates of labor force participation of metro, nonfarm nonmmetro, and farm women. Data from a large statewide survey (N = 5,880 women) conducted in Kentucky were analyzed to compare personal, socioeconomic, and family characteristics and the occupations and industries of women in the work force. Findings regarding correlates of labor force participation indicate that family and status are the most influential correlates of metro and nonmetro women's labor force participation, while status factors are more influential for farm women.

134. Bokemeier, Janet L., and Ann R. Tickamyer. "Labor Force Experiences of Nonmetropolitan Women." *Rural Sociology* 50, No. 1(1985):51-73.

Uses data from a statewide mail survey of nonmetropolitan households in Kentucky to examine characteristics of women's work, their job conditions, and financial rewards. Individual and structural explanations of labor market phenomena were used to identify correlates of women's employment experiences. Individual factors include sociodemographic characteristics and family status, while the structural dimension covers regional and spatial factors as well as industry and occupational variables. Results from multiple regression analyses suggest that the occupation and industrial makeup of the labor market has a major impact on women's work. Education is the most significant individual factor associated with work experiences, while age and family status have a lesser effect.

135. Bollmann, R. D. "Part-time Farming in Canada: Issues and Non-Issues." *GeoJournal* 6, No. 4(1982):313-22.

Reviews the phenomenon of part-time farming in Canada and discusses the identified concerns. Bollman reviews part-time farming in a historical context, then

discusses research based on the 1971 Census and recent
research on farm entry and exit. Policy recommendations conclude the article.

136. Bollman, Ray D. "A Comparison of the Money Incomes of
Farmers and Nonfarmers." *Canadian Journal of Agricultural Economics* 28(1980):48-55.

Compares farm and nonfarm income across Canada from
1963 through 1978 and addresses three questions: (1)
Has the farmer-nonfarmer money income gap closed in the
last decade? (2) What is the sensitivity of the
farmer-nonfarmer money income comparison to a change in
the definition of "farmer"? (3) What has been the
relative contribution of the net farm income and off-
farm income components of farmers' total money incomes
over this period?

137. Bollman, Ray D. "Off-Farm Work by Farmers: An Application of the Kinked Demand Curve For Labour."
Canadian Journal of Agricultural Economics 27, No. 1
(1979):37-60.

Develops the concept of a kinked demand curve for
labor to analyze the phenomenon of off-farm work by
farmers. It is shown that off-farm work by farmers is
consistent with a perfect market equilibrium and thus
that the existence of part-time farming does not
(necessarily) indicate inefficient food production.
The introduction of a nonzero cost of commuting to the
off-farm job indicates that the observed off-farm wage
rate may not be a good measure of the opportunity cost
of a farmer's time. In addition, it is shown that
policies that aim to increase farm firm efficiency may
cause an increase in the participation of operators in
off-farm work; underemployment may result from a
standard workweek that is greater than the desired
amount of off-farm work, and "hobby farming" may result
from a standard work week that is less than the desired
amount of off-farm work.

Refuted by item 166.

138. Breimyer, Harold F. "The Decline of the Family Farm."
Proceedings of the Academy of Political Science (item
229), pp. 186-97.

Examines current trends in the structure of agriculture and their political implications.

139. Brierley, John S., and Daniel Todd. "Agricultural and Urban Interaction in Southern Manitoba: A Canonical Analysis." *Canadian Journal of Agricultural Economics* 26, No. 2(1978):43-54.

Seeks to establish the degree of symbiosis or interrelationships that exist between agricultural and urban-oriented systems. Canonical correlation analysis is employed to analyze fundamental relationships within the basic rural-urban domain of southern Manitoba.

140. Brown, David L. "Comments on 'Rural Development: A Critical Perspective'." *The Rural Sociologist* 1, No. 3(1981):146-47.

Points out some shortcomings of the conclusions drawn by Lovejoy and Krannich (item 300) regarding the power of urban-based interests in rural areas.

Refutes item 300.

141. Brown, David L. "Implications of Population Change in Rural America." *Journal of the Community Development Society* 15, No. 2(1984):105-18.

Synthesizes research on the community-level implications of changing population size for the provision of services and facilities.

142. Brown, David L., Michael F. Brewer, Robert F. Boxley, and Calvin L. Beale. "Assessing Prospects for the Adequacy of Agricultural Land in the United States." *International Regional Science Review* 7, No. 3(1982): 273-84.

Reviews current information on the supply of and demand for agricultural land in the United States, describes the size and composition of the agricultural land base, discusses shortcomings of data by which use of this base is measured, and evaluates various estimates of future demands for the resource. The authors believe that available data and analysis provide only a limited body of verifiable information on the future supply and demand of U.S. agricultural land. This lack of adequate data and analysis permits

widely differing perceptions of the situation. Available empirical information, however, supports the
conclusion that a sufficient supply of agricultural
land will be available through the year 2000 to meet
both agricultural and nonagricultural demands.

143. Brown, Ralph J. "Simulating the Impact of an Irriga-
      tion Project on a Small Regional Economy." *Growth
      and Change* 12, No. 2(1981):23-30.

      Uses an econometric modeling technique to estimate
      the impact of a proposed large-scale irrigation project
      on a twelve-county area in southeastern South Dakota.
      The emphasis of the study is limited to the analysis of
      how a fully completed irrigation project would affect
      the economy; no analysis is provided of the construc-
      tion phase.

144. Brown, Robert W. "The Upsala Community: A Case Study
      in Rural Dynamics." *Annals of the Association of
      American Geographers* 57(June 1967):267-300.

      Analyzes the sequential occupance patterns of Upsala,
      Minnesota, a small rural community. The economic,
      social, and political organization of the community as
      a service area are explored.

145. Brozowski, R., G. Romsa, and A. Lall. "Some Factors
      Influencing Population Change in Rural Ontario."
      Scottish Geographical Magazine 89(1973):131-38.

      Tests the hypothesis that external influences play a
      more dominant role than internal factors in influencing
      village population growth. The relationship between
      such factors as size of place, occupational groupings,
      urban influence, and regional location and population
      changes of Ontario villages is examined for the period
      1941-1966. The analysis indicates that regional and
      urban influences are the most important explanatory
      factors.

146. Brush, J. E., and H. E. Bracey. "Rural Service Centers
      in Southwestern Wisconsin and Southern England." *The
      Geographical Review* 45(October 1955):559-69.

      Explores the spatial relationships in the hierarchy
      of rural service centers in Wisconsin and England. The
      authors conclude that the spatial hierarchy of central

places is related to distance factors that have a dominant influence in areas of low relief and fairly uniform rural population distribution.

147. Bunce, Michael. "Farm Consolidation and Enlargement in Ontario and its Relevance to Rural Development." AREA 5, No. 1(1973):13-16.

Points out that the Ontario Agricultural Rehabilitation and Development Act Branch relies heavily upon its Farm Consolidation and Enlargement program to stimulate rural development. Despite haphazard implementation and variable spatial impact, the program should improve agricultural conditions. Increased efficiency in farming, however, will create additional problems in rural communities and is unlikely to contribute significantly to general rural development.

148. Buttel, Frederick H. "Agricultural Structure and Rural Ecology: Toward A Political Economy of Rural Development." *Sociologia Ruralis* 20, No. 1(1980): 44-62.

Aims (1) to explore the causes or origins of rural environmental problems, particularly those related to structural changes in agriculture; (2) to demonstrate the profound linkages between agricultural structural changes, rural environmental deterioration, and rural underdevelopment; (3) to argue that a more holistic perspective, essentially a political economy, is necessary to fully grasp the important interrelations among phenomena attendant to the questions of rural ecology and underdevelopment; and (4) to suggest some useful strategies for change that can place the issues of agricultural structure and the rural environment in an integrated rural development framework.

149. Buttel, Frederick H. "The Political Economy of Part-Time Farming." *GeoJournal* 6, No. 4(1982):293-300.

Seeks to root the analysis of part-time farming in the political-economic structure of agriculture and the larger economy. While part-time farming is not a new phenomenon, the growing prevalence of part-time farming in the U.S. and other advanced industrial societies bears a strong relationship with the emergence of dualistic agrarian structures. Part-time farming has also been connected with the deconcentration of

industry and employment. The political implications of
the trend toward part-time farming are explored, with a
conclusion that multiple jobholding, while nominally a
"proletarianization" process, may in fact reinforce
political conservatism in the countryside. The paper
concludes by suggesting that future research on the
political economy of part-time farming should place
particular emphasis on the political implications of
and sexual division of labour on multiple jobholding.

150. Buttel, Frederick H., and Gilbert W. Gillespie, Jr.
      "The Sexual Division of Farm Household Labor: An
      Exploratory Study of the Structure of On-Farm and
      Off-Farm Labor Allocation Among Farm Men and Women."
      Rural Sociology 49, No. 2(1984):183-209.

      Explores the sexual division of on- and off-farm
      household labor using a random survey of New York State
      farm households. Interdependencies of average weekly
      hours of on- and off-farm work between men and women
      are examined. A preliminary empirical typology of farm
      men's and women's on- and off-farm labor inputs is
      presented that indicates the importance of conceptu-
      alizing family labor allocation patterns in terms of
      joint work role structures.

151. Buttel, Frederick H., and Oscar W. Larson III.   "Farm
      Size, Farm Structure, and Energy Intensity: An
      Ecological Analysis of U.S. Agriculture." *Rural
      Sociology* 44, No. 3(1979):471-88.

      Uses farm size, structure, and energy intensity
      characteristics of the United States to analyze the
      relationship of the energy intensity of crop production
      to farm size and structure.

      Refuted by item 217, which is rebutted by item 282.

152. Buttel, Frederick H., and Oscar W. Larson III.
      "Political Implications of Multiple Jobholding in
      U.S. Agriculture: An Exploratory Analysis." *Rural
      Sociology* 47, No. 2(1982):272-94.

      Explores two contrasting images of the political
      concomitants of part-time farming. Results indicate
      that, although part-time farming families in which the
      operator has a white-collar off-farm job are a particu-
      larly conservative segment among part-time farms, the

socioeconomic differences between full-time and part-time farmers are less than the differences within each category.

153. Campbell, Rex R., William D. Heffernan, and Jere Lee Gilles. "Farm Operator Cycles and Farm Debts: An Accident of Timing." *The Rural Sociologist* 4, No. 6 (1984):404-8.

Tests their hypothesis that farm operators more concerned with their financial conditions are those in the development phase of farming. The establishment and development phases are the times when most of the farm debts occur as the new farmer attempts to establish a viable farm.

154. Carruthers, Garrey, Billy Gomez, and N. Scott Urquhart. "Assessing Potential Commuting Mobility of Residents of a Rural Region." *Proceedings, Western Agricultural Economics Association 44th Annual Meeting* (1971):171-74.

Examines labor mobility through respondents' asserted willingness to commute in return for various financial rewards. Results do not substantiate a number of popularly held premises about the characteristics of potential commuters in a region. Over 600 residents of New Mexico were surveyed.

155. Cawley, Mary. "Part Time Farming in Rural Development: Evidence From Western Ireland." *Sociologia Ruralis* 23, No. 1(1983):63-75.

Examines the impact of off-farm employment on the rural economy by comparing full-time and part-time farms in an area of western Ireland. The implications of off-farm employment for patterns of farm and household expenditure and land use are examined.

156. Cheng, Juei Ming. "A Regional Analysis of U.S. Agricultural and Manufacturing Labor Market." *The Review of Regional Studies* 7, No. 3(1977):72-85.

Aims to identify and estimate the underlying structural demand and supply relations for farm and manufacturing labor forces on a regional basis, and to use these relationships in interpreting the wage disparities and labor supply conditions among the regions between farm and manufacturing sectors. The study uses cross-sectional data by state for 1950 and 1960 and focuses on the differences between the South and the rest of the nation.

157. Chicoine, David L.   "Farmland Sales in a Chicago Urban Fringe Market." *Journal of the American Society of Farm Managers and Rural Appraisers* 44, No. 1 (1980):20-25.

Summarizes market factors related to the transfer of farmland to urban use in an Illinois urban fringe area during 1970-1974. The focus is on the variation in price among parcels of farmland in Will County, Illinois, located in the Chicago rural-urban fringe.

158. Chicoine, David L.   "Farmland Values at the Urban Fringe: An Analysis of Sale Prices." *Land Economics* 57, No. 3(1981):353-62.

Explores the natural and man-made factors that affect the price of farmland in an urban fringe market, including factors not reported in previous studies. A hedonic price model is developed and estimated for an urban fringe farmland market near Chicago, Illinois.

159. Chicoine, David L., Steven T. Sonka, and Robert D. Doty.   "The Effects of Farm Property Tax Relief Programs on Farm Financial Conditions." *Land Economics* 58, No. 4(1982):516-23.

Estimates the effects of specific illustrations of use-value assessment and circuit-breaker schemes on the financial conditions of the farm operator and nonfarm landlord. The illustrative programs are contrasted with market-based assessments by simulating the financial performance of an Illinois grain farm over a ten-year period.

160. Clarke, G. J.   "Part-Time Cereal Farming." *Agriculture* 73, No. 5(1966):227-30.

Contrasts part-time farmers engaged in production of cereal (grain) crops with those growing such labor-intensive crops as strawberries, sugar beets, and potatoes. Those engaged in cereal production often are employed full-time off the farm and contract much of the farm work.

161. Clawson, Marion. "Factors and Forces Affecting the Optimal Future Rural Settlement Pattern in the United States." *Economic Geography* 42, No. 4(1966):283-93.

Defines an *optimal* settlement pattern as one which will offer maximum satisfactions to all people involved and at the least cost for the satisfactions obtained. A number of forces which affect the optimal settlement pattern are examined including changes in farm size and numbers, in farm marketing patterns, in purchase of farm inputs and items for home consumption, in use of town-based services by farm families, in economies of scale for group services, and in the quality of rural roads.

162. Clevanger, T., W. Gorman, R. Lansford, and J. Williams. "Selected Economic Implications of Alternative Development Strategies For the Navaho Indian Irrigation Project." *Proceedings, Western Agricultural Economics Association 45th Annual Meeting* (1972): 153-57.

Focuses on selected economic implications of alternative development strategies for the Navajo Indian Irrigation Project as reported in a recently published report. The specific objectives of this study were to identify the economic potential of selected crops and livestock and to specify and evaluate alternative farm organizational structures in terms of investment and operating capital requirements; income and employment created; and education, training, and skills required.

163. Conklin, Howard E., and William G. Lesher. "Farm-Value Assessment as a Means for Reducing Premature and Excessive Agricultural Disinvestment in Urban Fringes." *American Journal of Agricultural Economics* 54, No. 4(1977):755-59.

Examines the possibility that farm-value assessments can help to prevent premature and excessive disinvestments in agriculture in urban fringes--i.e., prevent the discontinuance or debilitation of agriculture before urban users are willing to make high urban offers for all of the farmland in an area. It is argued that the usual process for allocating taxes in urban fringes discourages the continuance of agriculture wherever efficient farming requires large real estate improvements that must be maintained and

occasionally replaced but lack value for nonfarm
purposes. Evidence from two New York City urban fringe
counties is used in support of this argument.

164. Coughenour, C. Milton, and Louis Swanson. "Work
      Statuses and Occupations of Men and Women in Farm
      Families and the Structure of Farms." *Rural
      Sociology* 48, No. 1(1983):23-43.

      Indicates that dualistic farm structure and
      increasing integration of the most populous category of
      farms (i.e., small farms) in the nonfarm economy are
      two of the most striking features of farm structure and
      that little has been done to study the effects of the
      multiple work statuses of adult family members on farm
      performance and the effects of off-farm work on the
      labor and capital processes of the farm business. Data
      from a 1979 Kentucky survey are used to analyze the
      relationships between farm acreage and sales and (1)
      type of farm family, as reflected in the farm versus
      nonfarm work statuses of men and women, and (2) the
      types of occupations and industries of those who work
      off the farm.

165. Coughlin, Robert E. "Farming on the Urban Fringe."
      Environment 22, No. 3(1980):33-39.

      Examines the supply and demand forces affecting the
      loss of farmland in the urban fringe. Various actors
      in the fringe land market are identified, and the
      effects on the land and implications for action are
      discussed.

166. Coyle, Barry T., and Ramon E. Lopez. "A Comment on
      Bollman's 'Off-Farm Work by Farmers....'" *Canadian
      Journal of Agricultural Economics* 29, No. 1(1981):
      93-99.

      Disagrees with Bollman's conclusions on two counts.
      First, these authors contend that hours of operator's
      labor per day of on-farm labor is invariant with
      respect to commuting costs only under unusual
      conditions on the farm production function. Moreover,
      these conditions are essentially inconsistent with his
      model. Second, they hold that an improvement in
      technical efficiency for an individual farm leads to an
      increase in off-farm employment only if the farmer's

production function and/or utility function satisfy unusual conditions.

Refutes item 137.

167. Cummings, Ronald G., Thomas A. Grigalunas, and Edmond E. Seay. "A Theoretical Framework For Rural Community Development." *Canadian Journal of Agricultural Economics* 22, No. 1(1974):58-64.

Outlines a programming framework which allows one to confront directly the issues involved in evaluating (as opposed to resolving) alternative strategies for rural community development. The model is designed to focus on the allocation of the community's limited resources among development activities, where the community's resources are specified within a qualitative, as well as a quantitative, context.

168. Davey, Brian H., and Zuhair A. Hassan. "Farm and Off-farm Incomes of Farm Families in Canada." *Canadian Farm Economics* 9, No. 6(1974):16-23.

Reports on the 1971 level, sources, and distribution of farm and nonfarm incomes and on the impact on incomes of socioeconomic factors such as age and educational level of the family head. Data are from a 1971 Consumer Finance Survey conducted by Statistics Canada.

169. Davidson, B. R. "The Effect of Agriculture on Country Town Population in the Grazing and Wheat Growing Regions of New South Wales." *Review of Marketing and Agricultural Economics* 44, No. 4(1976):147-64.

Attempts to identify the factors which determined the rate of growth of the populations of country towns in the grazing and wheat-growing regions of New South Wales between 1958 and 1971. The town population increased even though farm population declined during the period studied. In the Wheat and Sheep Zone and on the Northern Tablelands the rate of growth of country town population appeared to be determined by the rate of growth in the gross revenue from agriculture. In all other regions agricultural factors appeared to have little effect on the rate of growth of country towns.

170. Day, Lee M. "Research and the Family Farm: Implica-
     tions for Agricultural Economics Research." *American
     Journal of Agricultural Economics* 63, No.
     5(1981):997-1004.

     Examines the issue of the concentration of production
     on larger farms and the implications for research.
     Emphasis was placed not only on studies of the
     economies of farm size but also on agriculture-
     community relationships, particularly those dealing
     with the influence of changes in the structure of
     farming on rural communities.

171. Debertin, D. L., and G. L. Bradford. "Conceptualizing
     and Quantifying Factors Influencing Growth and
     Development of Rural Economies." *The Annals of
     Regional Science* 10, No. 1(1976):29-40.

     Develops a paradigm of relationships influencing the
     growth and development of rural economies. Causal
     relationships depicted in the paradigm are used as the
     basis for delineating a mathematical model which forms
     the foundation of an empirical analysis of forces
     influencing the growth and development of rural
     communities in Indiana. Alternative model estimation
     techniques are discussed, and empirical findings
     provide quantitative estimates of relative weights on
     forces influencing growth and development.

172. Debertin, David L., and John M. Huie. "Projecting
     Economic Activity Within Towns and Cities." *Journal
     of Community Development Society* 6, No. 1(1975):123-
     34.

     Develops and empirically estimates an econometric
     model to project economic activity in small- and
     moderate-sized towns. Sample projections are provided
     for two Indiana towns.

173. Deseran, Forrest A., William W. Falk, and Pamela
     Jenkins. "Determinants of Earnings of Farm
     Families." *Rural Sociology* 49, No. 2(1984):210-29.

     Points out that despite an increasing interest in the
     off-farm employment patterns of U.S. farm families,
     little attention has been focused on determinants of
     farm family earnings. Data on 1,772 husband-wife farm
     families from the 1977 Current Population Survey are

included (1) demographic characteristics, such as age, marital status, education, and previous migration patterns; (2) employment history and vocational skills and preferences; (3) participation in community organizations and activities; (4) marketing and trading patterns; (5) farm characteristics, such as acreage operated, principal enterprises, and type of business organization; and (6) financial characteristics, such as levels of assets, debt, and income and sources of credit.

188. Erickson, Donald B., and George D. Johnson. "Short-Run Determinants of Small Community Development." *Journal of Community Development Society* 2, No. 1(1971):39-47.

Uses factor analysis methods to develop a procedure whereby researchers can use a number of variables for communities to rank them with the other communities in an area. Kansas communities were used for this study.

189. Erven, Bernard L. *Part-Time Farming in Southeastern Ohio.* Socio-Economic Information Series No. 612. Columbus, Ohio: Ohio State University, Cooperative Extension Service, 1979. 2 pp.

Presents results of a survey of sixty-one part-time farmers in five southeastern Ohio counties. To be included in the study, the operator must have worked off the farm 100 days or more in 1976. On average, the respondents had worked 239 days off the farm. Net farm income made up only about 13% of their total household income. Few had expanded their farms in recent years, and only 10% planned to become full-time farmers in the future.

190. Ervin, David E., David L. Chicoine, and Paul D. Nolte. "Use Value Assessment of Farmland: Implications for Fiscal Stability." *North Central Journal of Agricultural Economics* 8, No. 1(1986):17-28.

Examines the possibility that farmland use value assessments (UVA) may create less stable rural tax bases in many states. Sources of instability include temporal variability in net farm income used to calculate UVAs, and institutional factors, such as data lags and averaging techniques.

191. Faas, Ronald C., David Holland, and Douglas Young.
      "Variations in Farm Size, Irrigation Technology, and
      After-Tax Income: Implications for Local Economic
      Development." *Land Economics* 57, No. 2(1981):213-
      20.

      Reports that locally retained income per acre
      generally decreases as farm size increases. Increased
      tax leakages from local economies are associated with
      larger farm sizes, due to the progressive structure of
      the federal income tax. Income comparisons presented
      in this study indicate that failure to explicitly
      account for potential differential tax leakages by farm
      size could lead to substantial bias in estimates of
      local and regional income associated with different
      farm-size alternatives.

192. Farquharson, Bob. "Trends in Number and Age of
      Australian Farmers." *Quarterly Review of the Rural
      Economy* 2, No. 3(1980):273-77.

      Examines changes in the number and age composition of
      Australian farmers between 1961 and 1976. Data from
      the Australian Bureau of Statistics (ABS) five-yearly
      Census of Population and Housing about the age and
      number of farmers and farm managers have been used to
      investigate the specific hypothesis that the average
      age of farmers is increasing.

193. Field, Donald R., and Darryll R. Johnson. "Rural
      Communities and Natural Resources: A Classical
      Interest." *The Rural Sociologist* 6, No. 3(1986):187-
      96.

      Reviews early rural sociology literature on the
      social and economic ties between a rural community and
      the surrounding region.

194. Findeis, Jill L., and Norman K. Whittlesey. "The
      Secondary Economic Impacts of Irrigation Development
      in Washington." *Western Journal of Agricultural
      Economics* 9, No. 2(1984):233-43.

      Examines the secondary impacts of two potential
      projects in Washington on the economy of the state. A
      major impact of these projects is to increase the
      energy costs to regional power consumers. After
      accounting for the negative impacts of rising energy

costs, the long-run state-level residual income increases by $209 million after irrigating an additional 700,000 acres. The distribution of potential benefits is uneven among sectors of the economy, and some sectors will possibly experience substantial decreases in returns to stockholder equity as a result of irrigation expansion.

195. Fischel, William A. "The Urbanization of Agricultural Land: A Review of the National Agricultural Lands Study." *Land Economics* 58, No. 2(1982):236-55.

Evaluates the data used as the basis of the National Agricultural Lands Study (NALS). Fischel contends that the Soil Conservation Service's survey data overstate the rate of urbanization in the past decade. He then presents three microeconomic models of urban expansion and concludes with a discussion of the NALS and anti-development interests.

196. Fitchett, Delbert A. "A Model of Irrigated Agriculture and Regional Development in Southern Argentina: The Rio Negro Basin." *The Annals of Regional Science* 8, No. 1(1974):14-34.

Develops a linear programming model to investigate some of the characteristics of alternatives rates of expansion of the irrigated agricultural economy of the Rio Negro basin in southern Argentina from 1970 to 1990.

197. Flinn, William L., and Frederick H. Buttel. "Sociological Aspects of Farm Size: Ideological and Social Consequences of Scale in Agriculture." *American Journal of Agricultural Economics* 62, No. 5(1980):946-53.

Discusses a number of ideological and value aspects of farm size; summarizes research on the social consequences of farm size and mechanization for farm families, nonfarm people, and rural communities; and advances several observations about political-economic aspects of farm size and their implications for the debate over agricultural structure.

198. Frank, Walter. "Part Time Farming, Underemployment, and Double Activity of Farmers in the EEC." *Sociologia Ruralis* 23, No. 1(1983):20-27.

Examines the status of part-time farming in the
nations comprising the European Economic Community and
proposes a new, socioeconomic classification of part-
time farming.

199. Friedland, William H., Amy E. Barton, and Robert J.
     Thomas. "Conditions and Consequences of Lettuce
     Harvest Mechanization." *HortScience* 14, No. 2(1979):
     110-13.

     Projects the conditions under which the iceberg
     lettuce industry would make the transition to a
     mechanized harvest system and the social consequences
     of such a transition. In addition to impacts on the
     character of the labor force and the impacts upon the
     communities surrounding lettuce production areas, labor
     force displacement could be as high as 87%.

200. Fuguitt, Glenn V. "Career Patterns of Part-time
     Farmers and Their Contact with the Agricultural
     Extension Service." *Rural Sociology* 30, No. 1(1965):
     49-62.

     Associates two career patterns of part-time farmers
     with contact with the Agricultural Extension Service,
     using a sample of farm operators in a rapidly
     urbanizing area.

201. Fuguitt, Glenn V. "Part-time Farming and the Push-Pull
     Hypothesis." *The American Journal of Sociology* 64,
     No. 4(1959):375-79.

     Tests the hypothesis that the extent of part-time
     farming is directly related to a measure of off-farm
     opportunities and, independent of this, inversely
     related to a measure of opportunities in agriculture.
     The hypothesis is supported by the analysis of all
     farmers aggregated and of commercial farmers; facts for
     noncommercial farmers are not inconsistent with the
     hypothesis in light of the low opportunities in agri-
     culture for this segment.

202. Fuguitt, Glenn V. "The Places Left Behind: Population
     Trends and Policy For Rural America." *Rural
     Sociology* 36, No. 3(1971):449-70.

     Is an analysis of population changes in incorporated
     places of the nonmetropolitan United States between

1950 and 1970. Size of place distributions have
changed little since 1950; however, the percentage of
places growing over each decade ranges from under 30%
to over 85% for different size and location groupings,
with smaller, more remote places less likely to grow.
A smaller proportion of places over 2,500 grew in the
decade 1960-1970 than in 1950-1960, whereas in the
South and in segments of the North Central region there
was an increase in the later decade in the proportion
of smaller places growing. Results indicated an
emerging decentralization trend around larger nonmetropolitan centers, and regions of the country showed
marked differences in some patterns.

203. Fuguitt, Glenn V. "The Small Town in Rural America."
     Journal of Cooperative Extension 8, No. 1(1965):19-
     25.

     Considers recent changes taking place in small towns
     (defined here as places with less than 10,000
     population), especially as they relate to population
     size. Social and economic trends in the setting of the
     small town are related to these changes, and possible
     courses of action for individual small towns are
     explored.

204. Fuguitt, Glenn V. "A Typology of the Part-time
     Farmer." *Rural Sociology* 26(March 1961):39-48.

     Presents a typology of the part-time farmer based
     upon past, present, and future commitment to farm and
     nonfarm occupations. The career typology is applied to
     data for 153 part-time farmers in Wisconsin. A
     necessary condition for the usefulness of part of the
     typology is demonstrated by showing types to be
     different on the basis of related occupational
     variables.

205. Fuguitt, Glenn V. "Urban Influence and the Extent of
     Part-time Farming." *Rural Sociology* 23, No. 4(1958):
     392-97.

     Examines the nature of the urban influences
     associated with the extent of part-time farming in a
     relatively homogeneous, prosperous farming area (forty-
     two counties) in Wisconsin.

206. Fujii, Edwin T., and James Mak. "The Impact of Alter-
      native Regional Development Strategies on Crime
      Rates: Tourism vs. Agriculture in Hawaii. *The
      Annals of Regional Science* 13, No. 3(1979):42-56.

      Examines the hypothesis that an alteration in the
      composition of economic activity in the form of a
      displacement of agriculture by resort development will
      increase crime. Authors use a cross-sectional analysis
      of the determinants of crime rates on the island of
      Oahu in 1975 and a parallel time series analysis for
      Hawaii from 1961 to 1975.

207. Fuller, Anthony M. "Linkage Between Social and Spatial
      Systems--The Case of Farmer Mobility in Northern
      Italy." *Sociologia Ruralis* 15, No. 1(1975):119-24.

      Reviews the nature of farmers' mobility between
      relatively distinct social systems in northern Italy.
      The upland *montagna* social system of the northern
      Apennines provides outgoing labor for the urban-
      industrial economy of the Po Lowlands, a migration flow
      which has many feedback characteristics. The impact of
      the feedback in terms of wealth and communication of
      ideas and values is manifest within the farm home, but
      is very inconsequential on the subsistence farming
      landscape. There is some evidence to suggest that
      feedback interaction between systems leads at least in
      the short run to the fossilization of the economy.

208. Furtan, W. H., G. C. VanKooten, and S. J. Thompson.
      "The Estimation of Off-Farm Labour Supply Functions
      In Saskatchewan." *Journal of Agricultural Economics*
      36, No. 2(1985):211-20.

      Develops a farm-household utility maximizing model
      which incorporates the time of both the farm operator
      and his wife. The model is then used to estimate the
      off-farm labor supply of the operator and his wife and
      to develop policy recommendations concerning further
      increases in off-farm labor participation by farmers
      and their wives. The results suggest that the supply
      of off-farm labor is inelastic for men but quite
      responsive to the estimated shadow wage for women.

209. Gardner, Bruce L. "Farm Population Decline and the
      Income of Rural Families." *American Journal of Agri-
      cultural Economics* 56, No. 3(1974):600-606.

Estimates the effects of farm population decline on median rural family incomes in states and counties. Farm population decline is found to be associated with increases in incomes of rural farm families and to have no long-term effect on incomes of rural nonfarm families.

210. Gasson, R. "Part-time Farming in Britain: Research in Progress." *GeoJournal* 6, No. 4(1982):355-58.

Overviews the current research activity on part-time farming in Great Britain.

211. Gasson, Ruth. "Farm Women in Europe: Their Need for Off-Farm Employment." *Sociologia Ruralis* 24, No. 3 (1984):216-28.

Speculates on the reasons why some farm women should seek work off the farm instead of, or in addition to, helping on the farm and considers some of the factors affecting their activity rate. Most examples are drawn from Britain and are supplemented with findings from other countries, mainly in western Europe.

212. Gasson, Ruth. "Part-time Farming and Farm Size." *Sociologia Ruralis* 7, No. 2(1967):176-89.

Uses evidence from several recent surveys of farmers in the United Kingdom to explore the relationship between the types of occupier and farm size. Since the long-term solution to the problem of the small farmer is to increase the size of farm, some reference is made to changes in farm size and attitudes towards change among full-time and part-time farmers.

213. Gasson, Ruth. "Roles of Farm Women in England." *Sociologia Ruralis* 20, No. 2(1980):165-80.

Describes the findings of a 1979 survey to document activities of English farm women, collect background information which might help to account for variations in roles, and explore any problems arising from the position of women in farming today.

214. Gasson, Ruth. "Roles of Women on Farms: A Pilot Study." *Journal of Agricultural Economics* 32-33 (1981-82):11-20.

Identifies three roles for women on farms. The main distinguishing features were division of labor between husband and wife, frequency of manual work, responsibility for farm enterprises, participation in formal organizations, and approach to housework. Reasons for women to play one role rather than another are discussed. Trends in agriculture suggest that the farmer's wife's contribution to the farm business will become still more significant in the future.

215. Georgianna, Thomas D., and Kingsley E. Haynes. "Competition For Water Resources: Coal and Agriculture in the Yellowstone Basin." *Economic Geography* 57, No. 3(1981):225-37.

Examines the competing demands upon water resources by energy and agriculture in the energy-rich Yellowstone River Basin. A mathematical programming model is developed to find an optimal solution to the allocation of the limited water resource among competing users.

216. Gessaman, Paul H., and Daniel G. Sisler. "Highways, Changing Land Use, and Impacts on Rural Life." *Growth and Change* 7, No. 2(1976):3-8.

Focuses upon measurement of the impact of highways by describing methods to estimate the extent and distribution of various types of land use in an area of New York's Appalachian Upland. The authors examine the trends toward increased urban penetration of rural areas and the impacts on rural life.

217. Gilles, Jere. "Farm Size, Farm Structure, Energy and Climate: An Alternate Ecological Analysis of United States Agriculture." *Rural Sociology* 45, No. 2(1980):332-39.

Illustrates some of the problems inherent in the use of Census materials by reexamining some of the data used by Buttel and Larson (Item 151) on the above topic.

Refutes item 151; rebutted by item 282.

218. Ginder, Roger G., Kenneth E. Stone, and Daniel Otto. "Impact of the Farm Financial Crisis on Agribusiness Firms and Rural Communities." *American Journal of Agricultural Economics* 67, No. 5(1985):1184-90.

Investigates the implications of the farm financial
crisis for rural communities--agribusinesses, main
street businesses, and the various community institutions, such as schools and churches. The article
focuses on impacts in Iowa and the upper Midwest.

219. Givan, William. "Some Observations on Farming in 1986
and Beyond." *Agricultural Economics Report* 2, No.
1(1986):16-29. Available from the University of
Georgia, Extension Agricultural Economics Department,
Athens, Georgia 30601.

Examines financial indicators for Georgia and the
Southeast, financial strategies being used by crop and
livestock farmers, and the role of off-farm income.

220. Goldschmidt, Walter. "Large-Scale Farming and the
Rural Social Structure." *Rural Sociology* 43, No.
3(1978):362-66.

Correlates the proportion of lower class population
with the prevalence of corporate farming, based upon an
analysis of the proportion of total state agricultural
production accounted for by the 31,000 largest farms.
Implications of the data are that, with the progressive
expansion of large-scale agriculture, the American
rural population will develop into a two-class system.
Regional variations are noted.

221. Gordon, John, and David Darling. "Measuring Economic
Growth in Rural Communities: The Shift-Share
Approach." *Southern Journal of Agricultural
Economics* (December 1976):73-78.

Identifies changes that have taken place in the
industrial composition of the local economy relative to
a reference area or standard of comparison (nation,
state, or region); explains differences in rates of
growth; and identifies industries in which the study
area has had a comparative advantage. Four Indiana
counties were studied.

222. Green, Gary P. "Credit and Agriculture: Some Consequences of Centralization of the Banking System."
Rural Sociology 49, No. 4(1984):568-79.

Examines one of the major trends occurring within the
commercial banking industry, the growth of multibank

holding companies. It is argued that a change in the
structure of the commercial banking industry toward
greater centralization through the growth of holding
companies will affect lending policies to farmers.

223. Green, Gary P. "Large-Scale Farming and the Quality of
Life in Rural Communities: Further Specification of
the Goldschmidt Hypothesis." *Rural Sociology* 50, No.
2(1985):262-74.

Reexamines the Goldschmidt thesis which has played an
important role in the recent development of the
sociology of agriculture. This paper uses county-level
data from a midwestern state to analyze two hypotheses
that are drawn from the literature on the Goldschmidt
thesis. The analysis is based on historical data for
the time period 1934-1978. The first hypothesis, that
the scale of farm operation would be negatively related
to the quality of life in rural communities, was
confirmed, with some important qualifications. The
second hypothesis, that the indices of quality of life
would be negatively related to the amount of increase
in farm size over time, received limited support.

Compare with items 54, 76, 238, 243, 490.

224. Gregor, Howard F. "Large-Scale Farming as a Cultural
Dilemma in U.S. Rural Development--The Role of
Capital." *Geoforum* 13, No. 1(1982):1-19.

Applies a multivariate model to county census data in
an attempt to propose a detailed and capital-oriented
definition of large-scale farming and outline its
geographic distribution.

225. Grisley, William. "Financial Distress on Pennsylvania
Dairy Farms." *Agricultural Finance Review* 45(1985):
1-10.

Examines the financial position of a large sample of
Pennsylvania dairy producers for 1983 and projects it
to 1985. Five different debt assistance programs are
investigated to determine the number of severely and
moderately distressed farms that would be assisted
enough to remain in business. The direct costs of
these programs to lending institutions are calculated.
Per farm costs ranged from $19,589 to $58,977 for the

severely distressed group and from $14,764 to $39,305 for the moderately distressed group.

226. Groth, Philip G. "Population Change in Counties Classified by Economic Function." *Growth and Change* 8, No. 4(1977):38-43.

Analyzes relationships among economic function, rural-urban character, population change, and net migration for counties in the North Central region. Groth presents a functional classification for counties.

227. Guttman, Joel M., and Nava Haruvi. "Cooperation and Part-Time Farming in the Israeli Moshav." *American Journal of Agricultural Economics* 68, No. 1(1986): 77-87.

Develops and empirically estimates a simultaneous equations model of the Israeli moshav (a cooperative village), in which levels of cooperative marketing, part-time and full-time farming, output, and capital stock are endogenous. This article attempts to fill a gap in the literature on the determination of the level of cooperation in agricultural cooperative villages, and the connection between cooperation and efficiency.

228. Gwynn, Douglas, and Orville Thompson. "Social Aspects of Water Resource Development: An Analytical Review of the Literature." *The Rural Sociologist* 3, No. 4(1983):233-42.

Seeks to complete a descriptive analysis of the literature on the social aspects of water resource development, to examine the general characteristics of the research itself and the way in which social research in water resource development is disseminated, to determine any regional variation in the frequency of studies, and to examine the degree of association between social research on water resource development and infrastructure investments in water projects.

229. Hadwiger, Don F., and Ross B. Talbot, eds. *Food Policy and Farm Programs*. *Proceedings of the Academy of Political Science* 34, No. 3(1982). New York: The Academy of Political Science. 250 pp.

Contains twenty articles about national food issues, government, and the future of agriculture. Specific topics are food policymaking, food stamp programs, hunger lobby, food lobby, conservation, taxation, energy policy, water rights, family farms, decentralization of agriculture, and the farm labor market.

Contains item 138.

230. Hady, Thomas F. "Differential Assessment of Farmland on the Rural-Urban Fringe." *American Journal of Agricultural Economics* 52, No. 1(1970):25-32.

Points out that urban pressures on farm real estate taxes led, in the 1960s, to adoption of differential assessment of farmland in at least sixteen states. Broadly speaking, the laws fall into three categories: preferential assessment, deferred taxation, and restrictive agreements. The laws are analyzed from the standpoint of both tax policy and development policy. In neither case is it possible, given the present state of knowledge, to conclude firmly that the laws are desirable or undesirable. The analysis does, however, suggest a number of potential problems which should be analyzed before decisions are made.

231. Hall, Bruce F., and E. Phillip LeVeen. "Farm Size and Economic Efficiency: The Case of California." *American Journal of Agricultural Economics* 60, No. 4(1978):589-600.

Examines the relationship between farm size and production costs. The analysis indicates that relatively modest-sized farms can achieve a major portion of the possible cost savings associated with size. The implications of this analysis were developed for the debate over acreage restrictions in reclamation policy.

See also item 359.

232. Hamilton, Joel R. "Population Change and Retail Sales Patterns in Local Authority Areas of Queensland." *Review of Marketing and Agricultural Economics* 50, No. 1(1982):97-108.

Uses census data from Queensland to test whether or not the relationships between population and retail trade patterns derived from central place theory were applicable at the local authority level. Larger local authorities achieve higher per capita retail sales than less populous places, and proximity to larger centers reduces per capita sales. Population growth allows a local authority to capture a higher proportion of spending locally, while decline encourages and even forces people to shop elsewhere.

233. Hamilton, Joel R., and Chaipant Pongtanakorn. "The Economic Impact of Irrigation Development in Idaho: An Application of Marginal Input-Output Methods." *The Annals of Regional Science* 17, No. 2(1983):60-70.

Uses marginal input-output to estimate the impacts of expanded irrigation in Idaho and to account for changes in input use from the average input mix of existing sectors. Attention is focused on the effect of new, energy-intensive irrigation on overall demand for electricity and on limited low-cost hydroelectric sources.

234. Hanson, Greg, and Jerry Thompson. "Farm Debt Capacity: Evidence from Minnesota." *Journal of the American Society of Farm Managers and Rural Appraisers* 44, No. 1(1980):13-19.

Examines the effects upon maximum debt capacity of the following six factors that may to some extent be controlled by farmers: management ability, farm size, enterprise diversification, interest rate levels, loan maturity lengths, and debt deferral in years of low income.

235. Hanson, R. J. "Nonfarm Income Earned by Commercial Farm Operators in Central Illinois." *American Journal of Agricultural Economics* 53, No. 1(1971): 103-5.

Measures the amounts and sources of nonfarm income earned by commercial farm operators in central Illinois. Total nonfarm income and amount by source are compared at different levels of farm and family earnings, age, and education. Off-farm occupations of farm operators and their spouses are determined, and differences in the characteristics of farm operations

were analyzed for farm operators who received wage and
salary incomes and for those who did not.

236. Hargrove, David S. "Mental Health Response to the Farm
      Foreclosure Crisis." *The Rural Sociologist* 6, No. 2
      (1986):88-95.

      Examines the response of mental health and social
      service agencies to the mental stress of farm
      families.

237. Harper, Emily B., Frederick C. Fliegel, and J. C.
      vanEs. "Growing Numbers of Small Farms in the North
      Central States." *Rural Sociology* 45, No. 4(1980):
      608-20.

      Uses a modified shift-share approach to analyze the
      resurgence in small farms (under 50 acres) in Illinois,
      Iowa, Minnesota, and Wisconsin. The analysis indicates
      that the growth in small farms is not strongly
      associated with specific other county-level variables.

238. Harris, Craig K., and Jess Gilbert. "Large-Scale
      Farming, Rural Income, and Goldschmidt's Agrarian
      Thesis." *Rural Sociology* 47, No. 3(1982):449-58.

      Extends Goldschmidt's analysis (of the relationship
      between the prevalence of large farms and the relative
      size of the "lower class" in farming) by adding an
      income variable for farmers, farm laborers, and the
      rural population as a whole. The model is a sequential
      ordering of five variables: farm-scale affects the
      farm social structure; these in turn affect the income
      of farmers, farm workers, and rural persons.

      Compare with items 54, 76, 223, 243, 490.

239. Hart, John Fraser, Neil E. Salisbury, and Everett G.
      Smith, Jr. "The Dying Village and Some Notions About
      Urban Growth." *Economic Geography* 44, No. 4(1968):
      343-49.

      Points out that most villages of 250 to 1,000 persons
      in the Midwest are not dying, but are continuing to
      grow in population, despite their obvious loss of many
      of their former economic functions. Based upon exten-
      sive field interviews in more than thirty villages

scattered over four states, and upon less highly structured field work in scores of other villages, the authors examine some of the implications of the fact of village growth for theories about urban growth.

240. Hassinger, Edward. "The Relationship of Trade Center Population Change to Distance from Larger Centers in an Agricultural Area." *Rural Sociology* 22(June 1957):131-36.

Examines the relationship between (1) the 1940 to 1950 population change of smaller trade centers in southern Minnesota and (2) the distance of the smaller centers from large ones. Results indicate that larger trade centers inhibited the population growth of the nearest smaller centers in the area.

241. Hauswald, Edward L. "The Economically Distressed Community: A Synoptic Outline of Symptoms, Causes and Solutions." *Journal of Community Development Society* 2, No. 2(1971):96-105.

Lists some symptoms of, causes of, and broad programs for dealing with community development situations that reflect particularly localized unsatisfactory economic conditions. As such, it is a checklist for lay practitioners of policymaking.

242. Hayenga, Wayne A. "Rural Bank Ownership Changes: Effects on Rural Communities and Implications For Agriculture." *Journal of American Society of Farm Managers and Rural Appraisers* 39, No. 1(1975):6-11.

Summarizes results from some recent studies about how bank ownership changes affect banking activities in rural communities with specific implications for agriculture. The main findings are from a Michigan study.

243. Hayes, Michael N., and Alan L. Olmstead. "Farm Size and Community Quality: Arvin and Dinuba Revisited." *American Journal of Agricultural Economics* 66, No. 4(1984):430-36.

Critiques earlier work by Goldschmidt concerning the California communities of Arvin and Dinuba. These authors suggest that many factors, besides differences in farm size contributed to Arvin's retarded community development. They believe that, rather than being

closely matched communities, the two towns developed
within significantly different economic, demographic,
and geographic settings. Thus, these authors contend
that, while Goldschmidt's hypothesis that large farms
accounted for differences in community quality may be
correct, his study of Arvin and Dinuba offers little
support for this assertion.

Compare with items 54, 76, 223, 238, 490.

244. Heady, Earl O., and Steven T. Sonka. "Farm Size, Rural
      Community Income, and Consumer Welfare." *American
      Journal of Agricultural Economics* 56, No.
      3(1974):534-42.

      Attempts to quantify the interrelationships of the
      welfare of rural communities and the number and size of
      farms. The impacts on farm commodity prices, the
      interregional distribution of production, net farm
      income (of the agricultural sector and per farm),
      number of farms, labor, income generated in the rural
      nonfarm and agribusiness sectors associated with agri-
      culture, and consumer food costs are evaluated and
      presented at regional and national levels.

245. Healy, Robert G. "How Much Urban Impact on the South's
      Farm and Forest Lands?" *Rural Development Perspec-
      tives* 2, No. 1(1985):27-30.

      Examines the recent and prospective population
      changes in the thirteen southern states from Virginia
      to Texas and explores the effects on the region's rural
      land base as urban uses take the better lands out of
      production. Between 1970 and 1980 the population in
      the South grew at twice the national rate.

246. Heatherington, Susan. "Potential Effects of Part Time
      Farming on the Household and the Rural Economy."
      Sociologia Ruralis 23, No. 1(1983):85-88.

      Examines four aspects of part-time farming in the
      United Kingdom: (1) the household division of labor,
      (2) rural employment effects, (3) linkages between
      part-time farming and other gainful activity, and (4)
      the potential role of part-time farming in alleviating
      farm structural and rural development problems.

247. Heaton, Tim B. "Metropolitan Influence on United
     States Farmland Use and Capital Intensity." *Rural
     Sociology* 45, No. 3(1980):501-8.

     Links change in certain aspects of agricultural
     structure to the concept of metropolitan dominance.
     Various explanations for increasing productivity and
     capitalization in agriculture can be attributed to the
     influence of metropolitan society on agricultural
     production. Confirmation of this influence has been
     sought by the examination of gradients in various
     aspects of agricultural organization, but recent trends
     suggest that the traditional gradient pattern of
     influence is being eroded by integration of a national
     metropolitan society. Gradients in two characteristics
     of United States farms (per acre value of farm products
     sold and per acre value of land and buildings) are
     examined at four points in time between 1950 and 1974
     in order to identify levels and change in the nature of
     metropolitan influence on these selected structural
     characteristics.

248. Heffernan, William D. "Sociological Dimensions of
     Agricultural Structures in the United States."
     Sociologia Ruralis 12 (1972):481-99.

     Reviews three major production systems (guild system,
     putting-out system, and factory system), which share
     many similarities to the family farm structure, and two
     alternative systems (corporate-integratee and
     corporate-farmhand structures). Results indicate that
     workers in the corporate-farmhand structure were less
     involved in the activities of the community than
     workers in either the corporate-integratee or family
     farm structures, but owner-managers of the corporate-
     farmhand structure were much more involved in the
     formal and political aspects of the community. The
     corporate-farmhand structure seems to suggest the
     development of two distinct classes for rural America.

249. Heffernan, William D., Gary Green, R. Paul Lasley, and
     Michael F. Nolan. "Part-Time Farming and the Rural
     Community." *Rural Sociology* 46, No. 2(1981):245-62.

     Suggests that the large and growing proportion of
     part-time farm families may have an impact on the
     nature of social relations in rural communities. The
     paper compares part-time and full-time farmers on the

basis of perceived community attachment, benefits
received from rural living, and goals and priorities
they have for the local community. These dimensions of
community life should give some indication of the
possible sources of conflict and strain in the rural
community. In general, the authors conclude that a
movement toward more part-time farming will have little
social consequence for rural communities which have
already been integrated into the larger urban social
organization.

250. Heffernan, William D., and Judith Bortner Heffernan.
"Impact of the Farm Crisis on Rural Families and
Communities." *The Rural Sociologist* 6, No. 3
(1986):160-70.

Presents results of a survey of forty-six Missouri
farm families forced out of farming for financial
reasons. The authors discuss characteristics of the
farmers, stress reactions and needed help, and the
consequences of unpaid debt on rural agribusinesses.

251. Heffernan, William D., and Paul Lasley. "Agricultural
Structure and Interaction in the Local Community: A
Case Study." *Rural Sociology* 43 No. 3(1978):348-61.

Examines the relationship between agricultural structure and social interaction through a case study of
grape producers in Missouri. Using both quantitative
and qualitative methodological techniques, information
was obtained for forty-one grape producers in a six-
county area. Findings support the hypothesis that
owner-managers of nonfamily farms are less involved in
community activities of a social nature than owner-
managers of family farms.

252. Hill, Frances. "Farm Women: Challenge to Scholar-
ship." *The Rural Sociologist* 1, No. 6(1981):364-69.

Assesses the current state of knowledge regarding
farm women's multiple roles as farmers, women, family
members, individuals, and members of agricultural
organizations. Hill offers suggestions for future
research and issues in research design.

253. Hirschl, Thomas A., and Gene F. Summers. "Cash
Transfers and the Export Base of Small Communities."
Rural Sociology 47, No. 2(1982):295-316.

Proposes an export base model of local employment
growth where one of the "export" sectors is cash transfer payments to individuals. The basic sectors
considered are agriculture, manufacturing, intergovernmental transfers, and cash transfers to individuals.
The model is tested with a sample of U.S. counties
using data from secondary sources. Cash transfers are
found to have strong positive effects on local nonbasic
employment growth. Manufacturing and agriculture were
also found to have significant effects. Also in the
model are ecological qualities, such as industrial
diversity and urbanization of the local community. The
findings and hypotheses are discussed in relation to
the population turnaround of nonmetropolitan communities, the growth of social welfare payments, the
economic significance of cash transfers to local
communities, and the Keynesian macro approach to
economic growth.

254. Hobbs, Daryl. "Rural America in the 1980s: Problems
     and Prospects." *The Rural Sociologist* 3, No.
     2(1983):62-66.

     Highlights some themes of the 275 recommendations on
     research and policy issues that were delineated in
     Dillman and Hobb's edited work (item 37).

255. Hodge, Gerald. "The Prediction of Trade Center
     Viability in the Great Plains." *The Regional Science
     Association Papers* 15(1965):87-115.

     Analyzes factors affecting the growth and decline of
     trade centers in Saskatchewan. Data were for the years
     1941 to 1961, a period during which extensive mechani-
     zation occurred in agriculture. A substantial decline
     in the number of trade centers was observed, and
     additional decreases were predicted. Small convenience
     centers located within 15 miles of a larger town were
     believed to be most vulnerable.

256. Hodge, Ian. "Forum: Rural Employment and the Quality
     of Life." *Review of Marketing and Agricultural
     Economics* 51, No. 3(1983):259-70.

     Points out that the nature of a person's employment,
     or lack of it, represents a critical factor influencing
     the quality of his life. The importance of employment
     arises not only from the income which work provides for

an individual but also from a variety of other attributes. This paper draws attention to the broader range of benefits which employment can generate and considers their significance in the context of some areas of rural policy.

257. Huffman, Wallace E. "Farm and Off-Farm Work Decisions: The Role of Human Capital." *The Review of Economics and Statistics* 62, No. 1(1980):14-23.

Presents some econometric evidence of the effect of investments in education and information (agricultural extension) on the off-farm labor supply of farmers. Data are county averages per farm for Iowa, North Carolina, and Oklahoma for 1964.

258. Huffman, Wallace E. "Interactions Between Farm and Nonfarm Labor Markets." *American Journal of Agricultural Economics* 59, No. 5(1977):1054-61.

Highlights some of the significant long-term changes that have occurred in the farm and nonfarm labor markets from about 1950 to 1975 and presents policy implications.

259. Ikerd, John E. "The Future of Family Farming in Georgia." *Agricultural Economics Report* 2, No. 1(1986):30-37. Available from the University of Georgia, Extension Agricultural Economics Department, Athens, Georgia.

Defines the family farm and examines its chances of survival. The author then discusses the fate of some full-time family farms that will not survive and what this implies for rural communities and agricultural policy. Although the focus is on Georgia, the discussion is in a national context.

260. Ikerd, John E. "Georgia's Agriculture in Transition." *Agricultural Economics Report* 2, No. 1(1986):1-15. Available from the University of Georgia, Extension Agricultural Economics Department, Athens, Georgia.

Examines changes in the following characteristics and trends in the agriculture industry in Georgia: number and size of farms, land use, cash receipts, types of farming, age of the operator, nonfarm employment activity, and ownership. The article concludes with an examination of farm financial trends and a discussion of future implications.

261. Infanger, Craig L., and Walter R. Butcher. "Individual Income Redistribution and Publicly Provided Irrigation: The Columbia Basin Project." *American Journal of Agricultural Economics* 56, No. 4(1974):805-11.

Examines the performance of publicly provided irrigation as a method of income redistribtuion by applying fiscal incidence analysis to a representative area in the Columbia Basin Project.

262. Jacob, Jeffrey C., and Merlin B. Brinkerhoff. "Alternative Technology and Part-time, Semi-subsistence Agriculture: A Survey from the Back-to-the-Land Movement." *Rural Sociology* 51, No. 1(1986):43-59.

Reviews the ideological basis of the movement, then describes the structural characteristics of a representative sample of 510 respondents. Focusing on the employment of soft, or alternative, technologies (passive solar heating, compost privies, etc.) as one case of back-to-the-land ideology, the study uses zero-order and multiple-regression models to predict alternative technological adoption and use. Personal values proved to be the best predictors of use of alternative technologies, whereas residential, family, and demographic factors were relatively poor predictors. This indicates that ideology is an important element in sustaining alternative rural lifestyles.

263. Jensen, Helen H., and Priscilla Salant. "The Role of Fringe Benefits in Operator Off-Farm Labor Supply." *American Journal of Agricultural Economics* 67, No. 5(1985):1095-99.

Focuses on the contribution of fringe benefits to off-farm labor supply by (1) examining the types of benefits received by persons working off the farm and (2) developing a model of operator off-farm labor supply which explicitly takes account of the fringe benefit component of off-farm compensation.

264. Jervois, Kym, and Jameel Khan. "Off-Farm Income in the Horticultural Industries." *Quarterly Review of the Rural Economy* 2, No. 4(1980):405-9.

Reviews briefly the importance and composition of
off-farm income in the horticultural industry, the
distribution of off-farm employment and investment, the
type of off-farm work done by the operator and spouse,
and the factors influencing the number of weeks worked
off the farm by the operator.

265. Johansen, Harley E., and Glenn V. Fuguitt. "Changing
     Retail Activity in Wisconsin Villages: 1939-1954-
     1970." *Rural Sociology* 38, No. 2(1973):207-18.

     Presents an analysis of change in retail and service
     activities in a sample of Wisconsin villages, documents
     trends in trade activities by village, and reviews the
     patterns of change by individual functions.

266. Johansen, Harley E., and Glenn V. Fuguitt. "Population
     Growth and Retail Decline: Conflicting Effects of
     Urban Accessibility in American Villages." *Rural
     Sociology* 44, No. 1(1979):24-38.

     Uses a path model and multiple regression to examine
     the relationship between urban accessibility and
     business change in rural villages. The weak associa-
     tion between urban accessiblity and retail change is
     due to a negative direct effect of urban accessibility
     on retail change being offset by a positive indirect
     effect operating through population change.

267. Kada, R. "Trends and Characteristics of Part-time
     Farming in Post-war Japan." *GeoJournal* 6, No.
     4(1982):367-72.

     Describes and analyzes the trend of and factors for
     part-time farming in Japan. Growth and expansion of
     off-farm employment opportunities, continued small-
     sized farming, rapid increase in farmland prices, and
     development and diffusion of labor-saving technology
     are among the major forces that encourage off-farm
     employment. On- and off-farm adjustments are
     discussed.

268. Kale, Steven. "Factors Associated with Population
     Change in Rural Areas." *Journal of Community
     Development Society* 7, No. 2(1976):41-58.

Employs a regression model to investigate the role of selected variables associated with 1960 to 1970 population change for 211 Nebraska communities with populations between 400 and 9,999 in 1960. Independent variables examined are urban proximity, size of center in 1960, government activities, traffic flow, manufacturing activities, farm density, community development, irrigation activities, and housing supply.

269. Kale, Steven. "Small Town Population Change in the Central Great Plains: An Investigation of Recent Trends." *Rocky Mountain Social Sciences Journal* 12 (1975):29-43.

Examines the areal pattern and spatial extent of recent small town growth and decline in the central Great Plains. Trends of population decline in smaller trade centers are noted.

270. Kelly, P. D., P. C. Riethmuller, and L. O. Dollisson. "Factors Associated with Changing Activity Levels in Rural Local Government Authorities in Southern Queensland." *Quarterly Review of Agricultural Economics* 31, No. 1(1978):151-67.

Examines interrelationships between rural and nonrural sectors and determines the likely spillover effects on regional economic activity that economic change might precipitate. This exploratory study is directed towards the identification of characteristics associated with changes in four indicators of regional economic activity--population, value of rural production, value added in manufacturing, and value of retail sales.

271. Kerachsky, Stuart H. "Labor Supply Decisions of Farm Families." *American Journal of Agricultural Economics* 59, No. 5(1977):869-73.

Analyzes the effects that an experimental negative income tax program would have on farm family labor supply given multiple labor market opportunities.

272. Kerridge, K. W. "Value Orientations and Farmer Behavior--An Exploratory Study." *Quarterly Review of Agricultural Economics* 31, No. 1(1978):61-72.

Examines noneconomic factors that influence the rate
of structural adjustment and the response of individual
farmers to adjustment pressures. The survey reported
in this paper was conducted in the Wheat-Sheep Zone of
western Australia and was designed to explore several
aspects of farmer behavior, particularly farmer value
orientations. The various value orientations held by
these farmers are related to farm performance variables
and personal characteristics of farmers, with the aim
of identifying factors influencing adjustment of
resources within the rural sector.

273. Kim, Joochul. "Factors Affecting Urban-to-Rural
Migration." *Growth and Change* 14, No. 3(1983):38-43.

Empirically investigates the factors affecting the
urban-to-rural migration phenomenon and provides
additional insights into the general direction of this
reversed movement.

274. Knoblauch, Wayne A. "Debt Payment Ability and New York
Dairy Farms." *Journal of the American Society of
Farm Managers and Rural Appraisers* 43, No. 1
(1979):29-34.

Reviews the procedure to calculate debt payment
ability, translates that ability into debt-carrying
capacity, examines the relationship of four management
factors which influence profits and thereby debt
payment ability, and analyzes the impact of interest
rates and the long-term to short-term debt ratio on
debt-carrying capacity of New York dairy farms.

275. Korsching, Peter F. "Measuring the Relationship
Between Changes in Agricultural Structure and Community Viability." *The Rural Sociologist* 2, No. 1
(1982):20-27.

Examines the problem of measuring the relationship
between change in agricultural structure and community
viability and offers suggestions for conducting future
research.

276. Korsching, Peter F., and Paul Lasley. "Problems in
Identifying Rural Unemployment." *The Rural Sociologist* 6, No. 3(1986):171-80.

Discusses definitional and methodological problems in identifying the unemployed in rural areas. Results from a 1983 survey of eight south central Iowa counties support their contention that the rural labor force is often underestimated.

277. Krasovec, Stane. "Farmers' Adjustment to Pluriactivity." *Sociologia Ruralis* 23, No. 1(1983):11-19.

Provides a brief survey of views and experiences of promoting rational adjustment of agricultural holdings to multiple jobholding in the process of rural development and farm structural change. The focus is on the peasant-like and semisubsistance holdings of continental Europe. Developments, such as mechanization of the holding, electrification of the home, better-organized marketing, improved and sometimes free transport to off-farm jobs, shorter hours, and a shorter working week in nonfarm employment, have helped to make the continuation of the modern part-time farm over several generations a practical proposition.

278. Kuehn, John A., Curtis Braschler, and J. Scott Shonkwiler. "Rural Industrialization and Community Action: New Plant Locations Among Missouri's Small Towns." *Journal of Community Development Society* 10, No. 1(1979):95-107.

Identifies community characteristics associated with new plant locations. The analysis focuses on new plants which located or relocated in Missouri's nonmetropolitan towns of less than 5,000 population during the period 1972 to 1974.

279. Lapping, Mark B., and V. Dale Forster. "Farmland and Agricultural Policy in Sweden: An Integrated Approach." *International Regional Science Review* 7, No. 3(1982):293-302.

Reports that Swedish efforts to retain farmlands are part of a more comprehensive policy to enhance the economic viability of the family farm. Aside from the containment of urbanization, farm rationalization is the major element in Swedish policy. Rationalization, which has generally meant the creation of larger individual farms, has allowed the family farm to achieve certain economies of scale and take advantage of technological innovations. The key actor in the

rationalization and containment process has been the
county agricultural board, a branch of local government
with unique and comprehensive powers to regulate land
markets, extend credit, provide technical advice to
farmers, and organize and manage farm amalgamation.

280. Larson, Donald K.   "Impact of Off-Farm Income on Farm
      Family Income Levels." *Agricultural Finance Review*
      36(1976):7-11.

      Finds that net farm income alone does not accurately
      depict the economic well-being of farm operator
      families. When classified by net cash income from farm
      sources only, 72% of all farm families were in the low-
      income group in 1970, but over half of these moved to a
      higher group when off-farm sources of income were
      included.

281. Larson, Donald K., and Thomas A. Carlin.   "Income and
      Economic Status of People With Farm Earnings."
      Southern Journal of Agricultural Economics 6, No. 2
      (1974):73-79.

      Focuses on loss-sustaining ability to analyze the
      change in economic status among people with farm
      earnings during the 1960s. In addition, the relative
      importance of each income source is analyzed among
      status groups. The results emphasize the importance of
      off-farm income in helping families move to higher
      status levels.

282. Larson, Oscar W., and Frederick H. Buttel. "Farm Size,
      Farm Structure, Climate, and Energy: A Reconsider-
      ation." *Rural Sociology* 45, No. 2(1980):340-48.

      Responds to criticisms by Gilles (item 217) and
      contends that his method of analysis is inadequate.
      Larson and Buttel provide additional evidence to
      support their initial conclusions about energy use in
      U.S. agriculture.

      A rebuttal to item 217 in defense of item 151.

283. Lasley, Paul, and Steven Padgitt.   "Farm Operators'
      Outlooks and Plans During an Agricultural Recession."
      The Rural Sociologist 4, No. 1(1984):19-27.

Presents and compares results of surveys conducted in 1982 and 1983 of 1,446 Iowa farmers. From a descriptive standpoint, Iowa farmers in August 1982 were very pessimistic about the outlook of farming and rural life in the decade ahead. By spring 1983 they were making few plans for purchases in the coming farm year.

284. Lassey, William R. "Impacts of Public Revenue Decline Upon Rural Services: Indicators from the State of Washington." *The Rural Sociologist* 3, No. 4(1983): 251-54.

Examines the effects of a decline in local, state, and federal revenues on expenditures for a range of public services in Washington counties.

285. Laurent, C. "Multiple Jobholding Farmers in Agricultural Policy." *GeoJournal* 6, No. 4(1982):287-92.

Presents results of an OECD study of multiple jobholding in fifteen of its member countries. Differences and changes in the way governments consider multiple jobholding are explained in reference to their own economic policy, which was influenced by natural and socioeconomic conditions.

286. Lee, Anne S., and Gladys K. Bowles. "Contributions of Rural Migrants to the Urban Occupational Structure." *Agricultural Economics Research* 26, No. 2(1974): 25-32.

Reports that rural-urban migrants in the United States do not appear to contribute unduly to the lower-status urban occupations. Nationally, their shares in 1967 were about equal to their share of urban population in the professional and managerial occupations, higher among craftsmen and operatives, and lower for clerical and sales people. They were represented proportionally in the service and nonfarm labor categories, and excessively among private household workers. Some differences in occupations of rural-urban migrants were noted for race-sex groups and for the South compared with the non-South.

287. Lee, John E., Jr. "Allocating Farm Resources Between Farm and Nonfarm Uses." *Journal of Farm Economics* 47, No. 1(1965):83-92.

Provides a theoretical foundation for explaining the
rationality of allocating traditional "farm resources"
to nonfarm employment. The model demonstrates the
conditions under which farm operators can combine farm
and nonfarm employment to maximize income and explains
the attractiveness of part-time farming as a permanent
or as a transitory organization of resource use.

288. Lefaver, Scott. "Rural Planning for Rural Communi-
      ties." *Cry California* 14, No. 1(Winter 1978-
      79):13-17.

      Discusses various ways agricultural lands can be
      preserved from urban development: traditional planning
      and zoning, planned rural development ordinances,
      planned residential variable density, "performance"
      zoning, use of scenic easements, transfer of density
      credits, and buffering rural areas.

289. Leistritz, F. Larry, Brenda L. Ekstrom, Harvey G.
      Vreugdenhil, and Arlen G. Leholm. "Off-Farm Income
      of North Dakota Farm Families." *North Dakota Farm
      Research* 43, No. 4(1986):39-45.

      Examines the magnitude and major sources of off-farm
      income for North Dakota farm and ranch families and
      evaluates the significance of nonfarm income in
      enabling these families to meet their financial obliga-
      tions. Information was obtained from a 1985 telephone
      survey of North Dakota farmers.

290. Leistritz, F. Larry, Arlen G. Leholm, Harvey G.
      Vreugdenhil, and Brenda L. Ekstrom. "Effect of Farm
      Financial Stress on Off-Farm Work Behavior of Farm
      Operators and Spouses in North Dakota." *North
      Central Journal of Agricultural Economics* 8, No.
      2(1986): In press.

      Uses discriminant and regression analysis to examine
      the effects of selected individual, family, farm, area,
      and financial characteristics on off-farm work behavior
      of farm operators and their spouses. Results support
      the importance of individual, family, and farm charac-
      teristics in determining off-farm work participation,
      but no consistent relationship was found between area
      characteristics (e.g., proximity to larger cities) and
      off-farm work. Financial variables consistently
      influenced off-farm work behavior.

291. Leistritz, F. Larry, Garland D. Wiedrich, and Harvey G. Vreugdenhil. "Effects of Energy Development on Agricultural Land Values." *Western Journal of Agricultural Economics* 10, No. 2(1985):204-15.

Uses multiple regression analysis to examine the effects of energy development on sale prices of agricultural land in western North Dakota. Objectives of the study were to identify factors affecting land prices and determine whether coal and petroleum exploration and development significantly affected selling prices.

292. Lesher, William G., and Doyle A. Eiler. "An Assessment of Suffolk County's Farmland Preservation Program." *American Journal of Agricultural Economics* 60, No. 1(1978):140-43.

Examines the farmland preservation program of Suffolk County, New York. The county passed a unique $21 million program to purchase development rights on 3,883 acres of farmland. Topics discussed are preserving a viable agricultural economy, maintaining an aesthetically pleasing rural environment, local tax savings, program size, and population growth.

293. LeVeen, E. Phillip. "Enforcing the Reclamation Act and Rural Development in California." *Rural Sociology* 44, No. 4(1979):667-90.

Investigates the relationship between farm size and the organization and nature of the rural economy and society with reference to the possible impact of imposing acreage and residency requirements. Alternative scenarios for enforcing the Reclamation Act are examined to illustrate how the original goals of the act might be obtained.

294. Lijfering, J. H. W. "Socio-Structural Changes In Relation To Rural Out-Migration." *Sociologia Ruralis* 14, No. 1(1974):3-14.

Focuses on the impact of the extensive geographic mobility of Europeans during the 1950s and 1960s, and on some of the consequences of this phenomenon for the socioeconomic structure of rural regions. Special attention is given to the consequences of international migration for the areas of departure, particularly as

far as these imply socioeconomic changes in rural
regions.

295. Lindley, James T., and Patricia A. Wiseman. "Some
     Fiscal Impacts of Farmers Home Administration Home
     Loan Activity on a Rural County." *American Journal
     of Agricultural Economics* 61, No. 1(1979):83-86.

     Examines (1) the percentage of borrowers who are
     natives (residing in the county when applying for the
     loan); (2) the real estate assessment of natives before
     and after obtaining a FmHA mortgage; (3) the tax delin-
     quency rate of FmHA borrowers relative to the rest of
     the tax-paying population, (4) the impact of interest
     credit mortgagors (subsidized through lower interest
     rates) relative to nonsubsidized mortgagors, and (5)
     comparison of per capita real estate taxes paid by FmHA
     borrowers as compared to the average per capita real
     estate taxes in the county.

296. Lines, Allan E., and Carl R. Zulauf. "Debt-to-Asset
     Ratios of Ohio Farmers: A Polytomous Multivariate
     Logistic Regression of Associated Factors."
     Agricultural Finance Review 45(1985):92-99.

     Describes an analysis of the relationship between
     debt-to-asset ratios and selected socioeconomic charac-
     teristics obtained from a sample of Ohio farm
     operators. The analysis was based on polytomous multi-
     variate logit regression. A statistically significant
     relationship was found between debt-to-asset ratio and
     operator age, farm size, and percentage of land farmed
     that was owned. No statistically significant relation-
     ship was found between debt-to-asset ratio and (1)
     major source of farm income and (2) off-farm income as
     a percentage of family income.

297. Lionberger, Herbert F., and Chii-Jeng Yeh. "The Chang-
     ing Influence of Clique, Neighborhood, and Church."
     Growth and Change 6, No. 1(1975):23-30.

     Examines how neighborhoods, social cliques, and
     church groups to which farmers belonged facilitated or
     restricted farm talk and information seeking in two
     Missouri farm communities over the decade from 1956 to
     1966.

298. Lively, C. E. "The Decline of the Small Trade
      Centers." *Rural America* 10(1932):5-7.

      Defines a small farm trade center as one to four
      business establishments. The decline in the number of
      such small centers in the North Central states over the
      period 1905-1929 is discussed.

299. Loftsgard, Laurel D., and Stanley W. Voelker. "The
      Consequences of Changes in Agricultural Technology
      for Rural Neighborhoods and Communities." *Journal of
      Farm Economics* 45(1963):1110-17.

      Points out that economic forces stemming from changes
      in agricultural technology have encouraged declining
      farm numbers and have increased farm size, leisure
      time, and mobility of rural people. The authors
      associate these and other changes with their effects on
      rural living in the Great Plains. North Dakota is used
      as an example.

300. Lovejoy, Stephen B., and Richard S. Krannich. "Rural
      Development: A Critical Perspective." *The Rural
      Sociologist* 1, No. 2(1981):84-91.

      Discusses various perspectives regarding the rural-
      urban dependency relationships.

      Refuted by item 140.

301. Lyson, Thomas A. "Husband and Wife Work Roles and the
      Organization and Operation of Family Farms." *Journal
      of Marriage and the Family* 47, No. 3(1985):759-64.

      Assesses how participation of husbands and wives in
      off-farm jobs is related to (1) various structural
      features of the farm unit and farm household, (2) the
      selection of a particular set of farm enterprises, (3)
      farm management practices, and (4) patterns of farm
      decision making. Data were collected from a random
      sample of South Carolina farm families. Discriminant
      analysis was used to articulate differences among four
      "types" of farm families based upon the off-farm labor
      statuses of the husband and wife. Results show that
      the husband's involvement in off-farm work is more
      important than the wife's in influencing the organiza-
      tional and operational characteristics of the farm.

302. McCarthy, Kevin F., and Peter A. Morrison. "The Chang-
      ing Demographic and Economic Structure of Nonmetro-
      politan Areas in the United States." *International
      Regional Science Review* 2, No. 2(1977):123-42.

      Uses multivariate analyses of county-level population
      change between 1960-1970 and 1970-1974. Two major
      conclusions were reached: (1) migration into entirely
      rural nonmetropolitan counties has accelerated and may
      be signaling a new spatial pattern of settlement, and
      (2) previous growth advantages associated with manufac-
      turing and government-related activity appear to have
      diminished, and retirement and recreation have emerged
      as important growth-inducing activities.

303. MacMillan, J. A., and J. D. Graham. "Rural Development
      Planning: A Science?" *American Journal of Agricul-
      tural Economics* 60, No. 4(1978):945-49.

      Discusses testing rural development planning with
      respect to (1) a proposed definition of rural
      development-planning research steps; (2) a summary of
      research conducted for the evaluation of the rural
      development plans for the Interlake Region of Manitoba;
      (3) applicability of the research steps for rural
      development planning in British Columbia; and (4)
      observations on rural development planning.

304. MacMillan, J. A., D. F. Kraft, and D. Ford. "Impacts
      of Agricultural Stabilization Programs on Development
      of Rural Communities." *Canadian Journal of Agricul-
      tural Economics* 24 (March 1976):159-77.

      Identifies mechanisms by which stabilization programs
      affect the development of rural communities, provides
      information concerning the likely pay-out and income
      distribution impacts of grain stabilization programs in
      the Prairie region, and describes the effects of
      stabilization on farm input purchases.

305. MacMillan, James A., Charles F. Framingham, and Fu-lai
      Tung. "A Proposed Simulation Method for Measuring
      Structural Change and Rural Development Program
      Impacts." *Canadian Journal of Agricultural Economics*
      22, No. 1(1974):26-41.

Points out that a number of agricultural development programs have been designed in Canada to increase agricultural productivity and improve incomes of low-income farms in marginal agricultural areas. A dynamic regional model of agriculture with an explicit linkage between the development programs and the regional economy (including rural and urban dimensions) is proposed.

306. MacMillan, James A., F. L. Tung, and John R. Tulloch. "Migration Analysis and Farm Number Projection Models: A Synthesis." *American Journal of Agricultural Economics* 56, No. 2(1974):292-99.

Examines alternative farm number projection models for the Canadian Prairie Provinces, including a synthesis of Markov transition probabilities and migration functions. The procedure indicates a potential for overcoming deficiencies of standard farm projection models. Explanatory variables include off-farm work, age of operators, capital, and regional economic structure.

307. Maddox, James G. "Private and Social Costs of the Movement of People Out of Agriculture." *American Economic Review* 50(1960):392-402.

Aims to identify some of the costs of off-farm migration and to draw a few conclusions about their relevance to policy formulation. The benefit side of the ledger is not considered. Attention is focused on costs which fall on the migrants themselves and which fall on the communities from which and to which they move.

308. Mage, J. A. "The Geography of Part-time Farming--A New Vista for Agricultural Geographers." *GeoJournal* 6, No. 4(1982):301-11.

Presents some theoretical and empirical research approaches to the study of part-time farming in Canada and addresses the potential contribution of agricultural geographers.

309. Maret, Elizabeth, and Lillian Chenoweth. "The Labor Force Patterns of Mature Rural Women." *Rural Sociology* 44, No. 4(1979):736-53.

Reports an exploratory study of patterns of labor force participation for two samples of rural women. Using data from the National Longitudinal Surveys of Work Experience, the authors investigate determinants of participation for rural women who live within the boundaries of SMSAs (Standard Metropolitan Statistical Areas) and for those whose residence is outside an SMSA. Findings indicate substantial differences in supply and demand factors related to labor market activity between the two groups of rural women.

310. Marousek, Gerald. "Farm Size and Rural Communities: Some Economic Relationships." *Southern Journal of Agricultural Economics* 11, No. 2(1979):57-61.

Determines the impact of structural change in the agricultural sector on the total economy of a community in Idaho. The author concludes that (1) small-farm operators had a higher propensity than large-farm operators to locally purchase both production inputs and consumption goods and (2) displacement of small farms by large farms results in greater regional income whereas increasing the number of small farms yields greater regional employment.

311. Martin, Philip L., and Stanley S. Johnson. "Tobacco Technology and Agricultural Labor." *American Journal of Agricultural Economics* 60, No. 4(1978):655-60.

Examines the benefits and costs which can be expected as a result of mechanizing the harvest of one of the most labor-intensive crops in America, flue-cured tobacco. Special attention is given to the magnitude of potential adjustment costs likely to be incurred by displaced harvest labor.

312. Mattson, G. A. "What Small Town Residents Should Know About Farmland Preservation Alternatives." *Small Town* 13, No. 1(1982):15-18.

Presents some traditional and innovative approaches to farmland preservation including zoning; tax agreements; transferable development rights; purchase of development rights; agricultural districts; and lease-back, landbanking, and fee simple programs.

313. Miller, Bill R., and Fred C. White. "New Evidence of Agriculture as an Underdeveloped Sector of the U.S.

Economy." *The Annals of Regional Science* 14, No. 1 (1980):43-56.

Develops an econometric interindustry model to quantify the linkages between the agricultural and nonagricultural sectors of state and substate economies. The results indicate that, at the margin, a majority of states are overindustrialized and underdeveloped in agriculture and that increased agricultural output without significant increases in costs would be relatively more important than additional production in basic industries.

314. Mogey, J. "Recent Changes in the Rural Communities of the United States." *Sociologia Ruralis* 16, No. 3 (1976):139-60.

Analyzes changes between 1960 and 1970 for all 3,000 counties of the United States. Results indicate that rural and urban communities share the same system of values and desires and that differences in opportunities to realize these desires through incomes and careers in farming account for much migration and change.

315. Molnar, Joseph J., and Peter F. Korsching. "Consequences of Concentrated Ownership and Control in the Agricultural Sector for Rural Communities." *Rural Sociologist* 3, No. 5(1983):298-302.

Discusses changes in the local economy, the social structure and politics, and the local institutions of communities affected by agricultural change.

316. Molnar, Joseph J., and Peter F. Korsching. "Societal Consequences of Concentrated Ownership and Control in the Agricultural Sector." *The Rural Sociologist* 3, No. 1(1983):34-41.

Examines the implications of the changing agricultural sector for society as a whole and for individuals who may wish to enter farming.

317. Morkeberg, Henrik. "Working Conditions of Women Married to Selfemployed Farmers." *Sociologia Ruralis* 18, No. 2(1978):95-106.

Reports results of a survey to determine the work
performance of Danish farm wives in their homes as well
as on and outside the farm.   Specific questions
addressed are as follows: Which groups of farmers'
wives have been drawn to the labor market, and which
groups will normally assist with work on the farm?
Which working conditions are connected with the wives'
work on and outside the farm?   What are the wives'
working conditions in the home?   How is the situation
of wives with regard to possibilities of child care,
holidays, and leisure time?

318. Morris, Douglas E.   "Farmland Values and Urbanization."
      Agricultural Economics Research 30, No. 1(1978):   44-
      47.

      Presents estimates of the effect of urbanization on
      farmland values and eventually food prices.   These
      estimates, which reveal a strong positive relationship
      between urbanization and farmland values, are used to
      construct elasticities of farmland value related to
      population density for the ten farm production regions
      in the forty-eight contiguous states.   These elastic-
      ities are generally elastic; thus, the author examines
      the issue of including a land charge in commodity cost-
      of-production budgets that could eventually be used as
      a basis for loan rates.

319. Morse, George W., and D. Lynn Forster.   "Agriculture's
      Contribution and Linkages to Ohio's Economy."
      Economic Development Notes No. 33(1985).   2 pp.

      Describes agriculture's direct contribution and
      indirect linkages to Ohio's economy.   Using employment
      multipliers from a state economic model, the authors
      report estimates of the total Ohio employment in
      support sectors required to supply inputs for Ohio's
      agriculture.

320. Moseley, Malcolm J.   "The Revival of Rural Areas in
      Advanced Economies: A Review of Some Causes and
      Consequences." *Geoforum* 15, No. 3(1984):447-56.

      Examines the recent growth of population in rural
      areas, particularly in Great Britain.   Two sets of
      explanations are examined: employment relocation and
      residential preferences unconstrained by job location.
      The paper then explores the consequences of these

includes a national sample of rural labor markets for an earlier part of the previous decade and an examination of changes within several Iowa labor markets.

336. Price, Michael L., and Daniel C. Clay. "Structural Disturbances in Rural Communities: Some Repercussions of the Migration Turnaround in Michigan." *Rural Sociology* 45, No. 4(1980):591-607.

Explores the structural effects of the migration turnaround on the small towns and communities of America. Perceptions of fundamental community problems were ascertained via questionnaires mailed to a sample of 21,792 Michigan households, randomly selected by counties. Findings show that the migration turnaround is linked to community problems, particularly in the areas of education, community solidarity, health care, social welfare, crime and public safety, and other municipal services.

337. Rainey, Kenneth D. "Forces Influencing Rural Community Growth." *American Journal of Agricultural Economics* 58, No. 5(1976):959-62.

Focuses on three questions: What is happening demographically in the rural areas of the U.S.? Can the recent growth trend be expected to continue? What does this imply as far as public policy and programs are concerned?

338. Raup, Philip M. "An Agricultural Critique of the National Agricultural Lands Study." *Land Economics* 58, No. 2(1982):260-74.

Focuses on the extent to which additional acres can be found or saved to meet demands that will be placed on agricultural land in the coming decades. The author discusses the benefits and shortcomings of the National Agricultural Lands Study in 1981. Problems associated with the interstate highway system, urban sprawl, and environmental degradation were the primary motivation behind the study.

339. Raup, Philip M. "Impact of Population Decline on Rural Communities." *Farm Policy Forum* 13(1960-61):28-36.

Contends that the population decline in small rural
communities is not due to the trend toward fewer and
larger farms nor the trend toward bigness in marketing
or retailing but rather is due to a lack of supervised
credit and agricultural research on surplus (nonfunc-
tioning) service communities.

340. Reynolds, John E., and Devin L. Tower. "Factors
      Affecting Rural Land Prices In An Urbanizing Area."
      Review of Regional Studies 8, No. 3(1978):23-34.

      Examines the impact of physical and locational
      characteristics of property on rural land prices in a
      six-county area in east central Florida.

341. Richardson, Joseph L., and Olaf F. Larson. "Small
      Community Trends: A 50-Year Perspective on Social-
      Economic Change in 13 New York Communities." *Rural
      Sociology* 41, No. 1(1976):45-59.

      Is based on a restudy of the thirteen New York
      communities included in the national sample for
      Brunner's three studies of 140 agricultural villages
      made in 1924, 1930, and 1936. The paper reports on
      changes in population 1920-1970; in Dun and Bradstreet
      business listings 1921-1970; in community boundaries
      1936-1974; in school district boundaries, in eighty-
      five community services and facilities and fifteen
      types of voluntary associations 1960-1974; and in
      industries 1964-1974.

      See also items 22, 23, 24.

342. Richmond, R. N., and S. I. Durbin. "Administration of
      Rural Adjustment Assistance in N.S.W." *Review of
      Marketing and Agricultural Economics* 45, No. 3(1977):
      101-8.

      Points out that a widening range of rural adjustment
      assistance measures is being utilized, thereby increas-
      ing the range of government organizations involved. In
      choosing between these measures additional government
      and nongovernment research is required, with proposed
      policies accounting for the division of responsibility
      for assistance that exists between government organiza-
      tions. There is also a need for greater policy
      coordination between these organizations. A proposal

for the establishment of a New South Wales Rural Adjustment Advisory Council is outlined.

343. Robinson, Chris. "The Off-Farm Income of Farm Families in the Australian Grazing Industry." *Quarterly Review of the Rural Economy* 2, No. 4(1980):400-4.

Examines the nature and extent of off-farm employment and off-farm investment as the major sources of off-farm income in the grazing industry and assesses the implications of drawing inferences about the well-being of farm families by reference to farm incomes alone.

344. Robinson, Chris, and Pat McMahon. "Off-Farm Investment and Employment in the Australian Grazing Industry: A Preliminary Analysis." *Review of Marketing and Agricultural Economics* 49, No. 1(1981):25-45.

Aims to document the nature and extent of off-farm employment and investment in the Australian grazing industry, to undertake an analysis to identify the factors important in determining both the type of off-farm employment undertaken by operators and the off-farm employment-investment strategy chosen by the farm family, and to present farmers' reasons for undertaking off-farm employment and investment.

345. Rogers, Susan Carol. "Owners and Operators of Farm-land: Structural Changes in U.S. Agriculture." *Human Organization* 44, No. 3(1985):206-14.

Discusses land tenure and transfer patterns in two Illinois farm communities as an example of the ongoing development, sociocultural influences, and intrasector variation within American commercial agriculture. Today, the dominant pattern in commercial agriculture is for farmers to own some of the land they work and to rent some throughout their careers, a tenure type termed "part-ownership." Although most farmers in both communities are part-owners, those in one community are shown to have more control over the land they work than do those in the other.

346. Rupena-Osolnik, Mara. "The Role of Farm Women in Rural Pluriactivity: Experience From Yugoslavia." *Sociologia Ruralis* 23, No. 1(1983):89-94.

Examines patterns and trends in off-farm employment
by women in Yugoslavia.

347.   Salamon, Sonya. "Ethnic Communities and the Structure
        of Agriculture." *Rural Sociology* 50, No. 3 (1985):
        323-40.

        Describes field studies of two ethnic farming commun-
        ities, one of German-Catholic ancestry and the other of
        Yankee ancestry, whose origin was in the non-Catholic
        British Isles. Despite similar farm soils and separa-
        tion by only 20 miles, significant differences exist
        between the communities in farm size and organization.
        The two communities studied are in the Grey Prairie
        region of south central Illinois.

348.   Salamon, Sonya, and Ann Mackey Keim. "Land Ownership
        and Women's Power in a Midwestern Farming Community."
        Journal of Marriage and the Family 41(February
        1979):109-19.

        Examines ethnographic data that demonstrate the
        organization of power within farm families and the
        manner in which this power is wielded in a central
        Illinois farming community.

349.   Salamon, Sonya, and Shirley M. O'Reilly. "Family Land
        and Developmental Cycles Among Illinois Farmers."
        Rural Sociology 44, No. 3(1979):525-42.

        Presents results of a field study among an ethnic
        community of farmers. Ethnographic data are presented
        to delineate characteristic traits of each type of
        family developmental cycle--expander families, conser-
        vator families, pragmatist families, and convertor
        families. The discussion focuses on family farming
        goals and the timing of retirement, intergenerational
        land transfers, and purchases of land. Survey data
        demonstrate a relationship between the age of the
        operator at the time of first land purchase and a
        family development cycle type.

350.   Sander, William. "The Economics of Divorce in the Farm
        Sector." *North Central Journal of Agricultural
        Economics* 8, No. 1(1986):1-6.

        Estimates the percent of farmers aged fifteen to
        fifty-four who were known to have been divorced in

1980. The divorce rate was positively related to the earning ability of farm women, particularly in off-farm market work. Also, an increase in farm family fertility reduced divorce probabilities while farm assets tended to be related with higher levels of divorce.

351. Saupe, William, and Priscilla Salant. "Combining Farm and Off-Farm Employment as a Farm Management Strategy." *Managing the Farm* 18, No. 7(1985):1-12.

Describes off-farm labor allocation among a sample of Wisconsin farm families and then assesses the implications of off-farm employment for the farm business and family. The basic information was drawn from a survey of 529 farm families in southwestern Wisconsin.

352. Scheuring, Ann Foley, and Orville E. Thompson. "Of Men and Machines: Technological Change and People in Agriculture." Part 2: "Changes in Hired Farm Labor and in Rural Communities." *California Agriculture* 34, No. 2(February 1980):7-9.

Discusses the ramifications of technological change in California farming from a sociohistorical perspective. Personal accounts are used to examine hired labor and mechanization and the changing rural communities.

353. Schmitz, Andrew, and David Seckler. "Mechanized Agriculture and Social Welfare: The Case of the Tomato Harvester." *American Journal of Agricultural Economics* 54, No. 4(1970):569-77.

Examines both social costs and benefits of mechanization, specifically the tomato harvester. The authors show that gross social returns to aggregate research and development expenditures were approximately 1,000 percent. Even if displaced labor were compensated for wage loss, net social returns would still be favorable. However, since compensation was not actually paid, it cannot be concluded that society as a whole has benefited from the tomato harvester. The authors make several suggestions for compensation strategies that would allow the social costs and benefits of technology to be more equitably distributed throughout society.

354. Schreiner, Dean F., and Marlys A. Knutson. "Place of
      Residence As It Relates to Female Labor Force Parti-
      cipation, Work Time Supplied, and Income Returns."
      Regional Science Perspectives 5(1975):125-53.

      Is primarily concerned with the role of place of
      residence in determining female labor force participa-
      tion rates, amount of work time supplied, and income
      returns for women 30 to 44 years of age. This age
      group is of major concern due to reentry of women to
      the labor market after the children are grown or in
      school.   Residence categories have been delineated as
      (1) SMSA-nonfarm, (2) SMSA-farm, (3) nonSMSA-farm, and
      (4) nonSMSA-nonfarm.

355. Schroeder, Emily Harper, Frederick C. Fliegel, and
      J. C. vanEs. "The Effects of Nonfarm Background on
      Orientation to Farming Among Small-Scale Farmers."
      Rural Sociology 48, No. 3(1983):349-66.

      Examines several hypotheses concerning small-scale
      farmers and the degree to which a farm background is
      related to identification with farming, farm
      activities, agrarian value orientations, and attitudes
      toward local agricultural service agencies.   The
      question that is addressed is whether or not those
      without farm backgrounds have a different orientation
      to farming than those who grew up on farms. Data for
      the analysis were obtained from a 1980 survey of 348
      small farmers in Illinois.

356. Schwarzweller, H. K.   "Part-time Farming in Australia:
      Research in Progress." *GeoJournal* 6, No. 4(1982):
      281-82.

      Overviews the current research activity on part-time
      farming in Australia.

357. Scott, Loren C., Lewis H. Smith, and Brian Rungeling.
      "Labor Force Participation in Southern Rural Labor
      Markets." *American Journal of Agricultural Economics*
      59, No. 2(1977):266-74.

      Investigates the major determinants of labor force
      participation among six subgroups by employing primary
      data from interviews conducted in four southern rural
      counties. Evidence from probit analysis indicates the
      critical role of health in the participation decision

of virtually all subgroups. The expected wage is found to significantly influence the participation decision of secondary, but not primary, workers. Manpower policies involving day-care centers, discrimination, and job training are also investigated.

358. Seastone, Don. "The Regional Dependency Effect of Federal Land Ownership." *Land Economics* 46, No. 4(1970):394-403.

Develops the thesis that elements of federal land policy have resulted in a pattern of land ownership that leaves federal-land-intensive regions critically dependent upon land use decisions of land management agencies rather than upon ordinary market forces. This dependency, in turn, becomes a crucial determinant of the rate of regional economic growth and the direction of economic development.

359. Seckler, David, and Robert A. Young. "Economic and Policy Implications of the 160-Acre Limitation in Federal Reclamation Law." *American Journal of Agricultural Economics* 60, No. 4(1978):575-88.

Examines the controversy over the 160-acre limitation in federal irrigation projects. The discussion attempts to review the status of federal water programs with respect to the acreage limitation and with particular reference to the Westlands and Imperial Water Districts in California.

360. Shaudys, E. T. "Preferential Taxation of Farmland: The Ohio Experience." *Journal of the American Society of Farm Managers and Rural Appraisers* 44, No. 1(1980):36-45.

Reviews the land use control system in Ohio in an attempt to understand why a preferential taxation of farmland was enacted. Ohio has been under urban-related pressures to develop land use controls.

361. Shaw, R. Paul. "Canadian Farm and Nonfarm Family Incomes." *American Journal of Agricultural Economics* 61, No. 4(1979):676-82.

Utilizes an improved data base, formed through linkage of Canada's 1971 Censuses of Agriculture and Population, to (1) analyze disparities in farm and urban incomes in Canada and (2) identify the impact that off-farm work has in reducing these disparities.

362. Simpson, Wayne, and Marilyn Kapitany. "The Off-Farm Work Behavior of Farm Operators." *American Journal of Agricultural Economics* 65, No. 4(1983):801-5.

Develops two formal models of off-farm labor supply. First, off-farm work decisions are analyzed in a conventional utility-maximizing framework consistent with the view that off-farm work is chosen when marginal returns to farming fall below potential off-farm returns. The second model analyzes the off-farm work decision when an income target, reflecting the need to meet the financial obligations of farming, is the objective.

363. Singh, Surendra. "Part-Time Farm Operators and Supply of Off-Farm Labor By Farm Operators in Rural Areas." *Journal of the Community Development Society* 14, No. 1(1983):51-61.

Examines major characteristics of selected part-time farmers and analyzes factors affecting off-farm supply of labor by farm operators. The paper reports results of a study of 193 randomly selected farm families in two counties of west Tennessee. Part-time farmers were found to be relatively younger, more educated, to have a higher total family income, and to be operating smaller farms, as compared to full-time farmers.

364. Singh, Surendra P., and Handy Williamson, Jr. "Part-time Farming: Productivity and Some Implications of Off-farm Work by Farmers." *Southern Journal of Agricultural Economics* 13, No. 2 (1981):61-67.

Determines possible differences between production functions on part-time and full-time farms; determines differences in productivity levels as means to appraise resource allocative efficiency; and discusses some implications of off-farm work by farmers. Results indicate that, although part-time and full-time farms exhibit significant differences, part-time farms are no less efficient in their allocation of resources or in the production of food.

365. Smith, Arthur H., and William E. Martin. "Socioeconomic Behavior of Cattle Ranchers, with Implications

For Rural Community Development in the West." *American Journal of Agricultural Economics* 54, No. 2(1972):217-25.

Extends the argument that cattle ranching and ranchers can be better understood by viewing the ranch resource as generating both production and consumption outputs. It was found that nonmonetary outputs of ranch ownership are the most significant factors in explaining high sale prices of Arizona ranches. Land fundamentalism, rural fundamentalism, and conspicuous consumption/speculative attitudes are the most important of these consumption outputs. The analysis suggests that small town viability and growth in the arid Southwest, and possibly in the West as a whole, may be more likely to occur if rural development policies are not predicated on the economic impact of surrounding ranches.

366. Smith, Eldon D., Brady Deaton, and David Kelch. "Cost-Effective Programs of Rural Community Industrialization." *Journal of Community Development Society* 11, No. 1(1980):113-23.

Provides information about industrial potentials for rural communities and helps to identify effective industrial development program directions. Data are from a study of 565 incorporated nonmetropolitan communities in Kentucky and Tennessee for the period 1970-73.

367. Smith, Stephen M., and Glen C. Pulver. "Nonmanufacturing Business as a Growth Alternative in Nonmetropolitan Areas." *Journal of Community Development Society* 12, No. 1(1981):33-47.

Provides information on the nonmanufacturing business sector and recommends it as an alternative to small towns trying to provide more employment opportunities. Four characteristics of these businesses are described: size of businesses as measured by employment, level of linkages to the local economy, types of ownership structure, and factors which favor or hinder location and operation in nonmetropolitan communities.

368. Smith, T. Lynn. "Sociocultural Changes in 12 Midwestern Communities, 1930-1970." *Social Science* 49, No. 4(1974):195-207.

Summarizes demographic and related changes in communities in Indiana, Minnesota, and North Dakota over a 40-year period. Salient trends noted by the author include (1) a rapid increase in the number and proportion of aged persons, (2) a tendency for females to increasingly outnumber males, and (3) an inordinately high proportion of widows among the residents. Changes in these communities are related to changes in agriculture, transportation, and communication.

369. Sofranko, Andrew J., and Frederick C. Fliegel. "The Neglected Component of Rural Population Growth." *Growth and Change* 14, No. 2(1983):42-49.

Examines two research issues: (1) whether and to what extent migrants originating in rural and urban residence areas have different characteristics and motivation, and (2) whether as a function of their origins they are likely to have different impacts on rural growth areas. Seventy-five rapidly growing counties in the Midwest are the focus of the study.

370. Sonka, Steven T., and Earl O. Heady. "Effects of Alternative Farm Policies on Farm and Nonfarm Sectors of Rural America." *Southern Journal of Agricultural Economics* 6, No. 2(1974):47-58.

Attempts to quantitatively measure the impact of alternative government farm policies not only on commercial agriculture but also on the communities and industries that exist to serve it. Policy alternatives examined include a free market alternative, a land retirement program, and two programs featuring production quotas.

371. Steeves, Allan D. "Mobility Into and Out of Canadian Agriculture." *Rural Sociology* 44, No. 3(1979):566-83.

Uses 1966, 1971, and 1976 Agricultural Censuses to analyze the gross rates of entry into and exit from farming. There were wide variations in rates of gross entry and exit among various Canadian provinces, different types of enterprises, total capital values of the farm investment, gross farm sales, age of operator, and days worked off the farm. The magnitude and character of these differences are discussed in the context of the dynamics of farm labor markets in highly industrialized societies.

372. Stockdale, Jerry D. "Technology and Change In United States Agriculture: Model or Warning?" *Sociologia Ruralis* 17, No. 1(1977):43-58.

Points out that rapid increases in productivity of U.S. agriculture have been accompanied by large decreases in the number of farms and in persons employed and/or living on farms. The decline in farm employment and population has, in turn, had a devastating impact on many rural communities. In many nonmetropolitan communities, the number of businesses serving agriculture has declined, and retail firms have suffered. In many such communities the quality of private services available locally has declined, and the ability to support public services has decreased.

373. Stoddard, Ellwyn R. "Dairy Farmers on Strike: Farm Bargaining Attitudes As Influenced by Off-Farm Work Experience." *Rural Sociology* 36, No. 3(1971):379-88.

Investigates the impact of union membership and industrial work experience on the attitudes of part-time farmers toward applying urban proletarian techniques to their farming operations. The study was conducted among Michigan dairy farmers following the Detroit milk strike of 1956.

374. Stoevener, Herbert H., and Roger G. Kraynick. "On Augmenting Community Economic Performance by New or Continuing Irrigation Developments." *American Journal of Agricultural Economics* 61, No. 5(1979):1115-23.

Examines the nature and extent of regional development impacts of irrigation development. The authors identify some of the major policy issues involved, classify relevant empirical studies on this subject, and make some suggestions for research approaches.

375. Sumner, Daniel A. "The Off-Farm Labor Supply of Farmers." *American Journal of Agricultural Economics* 64, No. 3(1982):499-509.

Develops theoretical and empirical models to examine the off-farm wages, labor force participation, and hours of work of farmers. Econometric estimates are based on data from a 1971 survey of Illinois farmers. The off-farm wage depends on farmer's human capital and the local labor market. The major result confirms the sensitivity of off-farm work to economic incentives. A 10% increase in the off-farm wage entails an 11% increase in hours of off-farm work when farm characteristics are held constant. Results also indicate effects of seasonality, risk, and life cycle factors on off-farm work.

376. Swanson, Louis E., and Lawrence Busch. "A Part-time Farming Model Reconsidered: A Comment on a POET Model." *Rural Sociology* 50, No. 3(1985):427-36.

Evaluates the methodology, conceptual framework, and conclusions of the Albrecht and Murdock article.

Refutes item 118; rebutted by item 116.

377. Sweet, James A. "The Employment of Rural Farm Wives." *Rural Sociology* 37, No. 4(1972):553-77.

Uses multivariate analysis to examine the employment patterns of rural farm wives. Employment differentials among rural farm wives are compared with those among urban wives. Some speculation is offered on the reasons for the observed regional, racial, and educational differentials in employment and for the lack of an effect of other family income on employment. An attempt is made to differentiate the farm population according to husband's occupation, tenure of housing, and source of income (self-employment vs. wage and salary), and to examine differential patterns of the wife's employment.

378. Symes, D. G. "Part-time Farming in Norway." *GeoJournal* 6, No. 4 (1982):351-54.

Examines the trend of Norwegian farmers to hold part-time urban, industrial jobs. Sources of nonfarm income are discussed along with the decline of the farming-fishing way of life.

379. Tarver, James D. "Patterns of Population Change Among Southern Nonmetropolitan Towns, 1950-1970." *Rural Sociology* 37, No. 1(1972):53-72.

Relates the patterns of population growth and decline to the industrial structure of southern nonmetropolitan towns and cities. Analyzed were the 1950-1960, 1960-1970, and 1950-1970 population changes of the 789 southern nonmetropolitan towns that had between 2,500 and 9,999 inhabitants in 1950 and were separately enumerated in the 1960 and 1970 censuses of population. This study shows that the industrial structure of towns at the beginning of a decade exerted a pronounced influence upon the population trends during the ensuing decade. Agricultural centers, which had the highest relative population increases of all types of one-specialty towns from 1950 to 1960, suffered the greatest proportionate population declines from 1960 to 1970.

380. Tauriainen, Juhani, and Frank W. Young. "The Impact of Urban-Industrial Development on Agricultural Incomes and Productivity in Finland." *Land Economics* 52, No. 2(1976):192-206.

Tests the so-called urban-industrial impact hypothesis, which suggests that farm incomes and productivity are highest near centers of urban-industrial development. Regression analysis using data from Finnish communes for the period 1960 to 1970 does not negate the hypothesis in any fundamental way; however, the findings demonstrate the need to measure this impact at the regional level and with measures that are sensitive to the urban aspects of central places as well as to industrial development.

381. Thurmeir, Margie. "The Determinants of Off-Farm Employment of Saskatchewan Farmers." *Canadian Journal of Agricultural Economics* 29-30(1981-82): 339-48.

Develops and tests a model of off-farm employment. Variables that decrease the amount of operator's labor needed on the farm are found to positively affect off-farm employment. Increases in wage rates also have a positive effect, but years of farming experience have a negative influence.

382. Tubman, Wendy. "A Note on Off-Farm Income of Farm Families In Australia." *Australian Journal of Agricultural Economics* 21, No. 3(1977):209-14.

Aims to collate and examine the degree to which farm labor resources are employed in off-farm activities in Australia. The main conclusion drawn from the evidence available is that, while in aggregate part-time farming is a fairly minor activity, in some sectors it is increasing in importance and constitutes a considerable outlet for farm-based labor resources.

383. Tweeten, Luther. "Agricultural and Rural Development in the 1980s and Beyond." *Western Journal of Agricultural Economics* 8, No. 2(1983):230-40.

Examines the economic forces shaping agriculture and rural communities to ascertain some indication of the future of these communities. Tweeten concludes that rural communities are now highly integrated into national and international markets and public policies and that farmers increasingly depend on the nonfarm sector for production inputs and off-farm jobs. Two principal problems of the farming industry appear to be (1) instability caused by nature, politics, and business cycles at home and abroad, and (2) cash-flow problems induced by inflation or high real interest rates, and by high cash costs of farm operation, ownership, and consumption.

384. Tweeten, Luther. "The Economics of Small Farms." *Science* 219, No. 4588(March 4, 1983):1037-41.

Examined and found no evidence to accept the following hypotheses about small farms (with receipts under $40,000 per year): (1) small farms provide a higher quality of life to operators and their families than do larger farms; (2) small farm operators take better care of their soil; (3) small farms are more energy efficient; (4) small farm preservation and encouragement avoids the trauma of outmigration of farm people to cities; (5) society would be better off if publicly supported research and extension education were focused on small farms; (6) federal government programs have hastened the demise of small farms; (7) small farms provide the social and economic support necessary to maintain vitality of nearby towns and cities; and (8) preservation of small farms is essential to economic competition because it avoids concentrating production on a few large farms which would practice monopoly pricing and raise food costs.

385. Tweeten, Luther. "Impact of Federal Fiscal-Monetary Policy on Farm Structure." *Western Journal of Agricultural Economics* 8, No. 1(1983):61-69.

Examines the impact of federal fiscal-monetary policies, which influence aggregate demand, on farm structure (i.e., farm size and numbers, tenure, legal organization, investment, capital-labor ratio, productivity, and status--part-time or full-time). Tweeten concludes that favorable policies cause income and technology to grow, and unfavorable policies tilt comparative advantage to established family farms, renters (including part owners), corporate industrial-conglomerate farms, and part-time small farms.

386. van Blokland, P. J. "A Perspective on the Current Agricultural Financial Crisis." *Farm Management News and Views.* Mississippi State, Mississippi: Mississippi State University, Cooperative Extension Service, May 1985. 4 pp.

Discusses the causes and severity of the current financial crisis in agriculture and offers some solutions, including exchanging debt for equity capital, export subsidies, and education.

387. vanVuuren, Willem, and John R. Cummings. "The Impact of Housing Development in Rural Areas on Farm Property Taxes." *Canadian Journal of Agricultural Economics* 26, No. 3(1978):31-37.

Examines the effect of nonfarm housing development in rural areas of Ontario on the local tax base, tax rates, and levels of services.

388. Visser, Sent. "Technological Change and the Spatial Structure of Agriculture." *Economic Geography* 56, No. 4(1980):311-19.

Tests von Thunen's theory of agricultural location which indicates that agricultural intensity should decrease at a decreasing rate as distance to market increases. A regression analysis using Great Plains data reveals that capital-using technological change was specific to certain farming types whose location was not a function of global market access. Those types were irrigated farming, pastoral farming, and farming in the vicinity of local SMSAs.

389. Voth, Donald E., and Diana M. Danforth. "Effect of
      Schools upon Small Community Growth and Decline."
      The Rural Sociologist 1, No. 6(1981):364-69.

      Attempts to determine whether change in the presence
      or absence of rural schools and in the number of
      schools operating in a local community could be demon-
      strated to influence community growth.

390. Walzer, Norman, and David Schmidt. "Population Change
      and Retail Sales in Small Communities." *Growth and
      Change* 8, No. 1(1977):45-49.

      Reports on the probability of population decreases
      during the 1960s in midwestern communities grouped by
      size and proximity to larger urban areas. Also
      reported is an analysis of the socioeconomic factors
      associated with the level of per capita retail sales in
      eighty-six Illinois communities of between 2,500 and
      10,000 population.

391. Whitener, Leslie, ed. "Farmwomen's Contributions to
      Agriculture and the Rural Economy." Contributing
      authors are Carolyn Sachs, Peggy J. Ross, Judith Z.
      Kalbacher, and Priscilla Salant. *Rural Development
      Perspectives* 1, No. 2(1985):20-26.

      Explores the changing role of women in agriculture
      and their contribution to the rural economy. Salant
      examines off-farm work activity of farm women.

392. Wibberley, Gerald. "Rural Resource Development in
      Britain and Environmental Concern." *Journal of Agri-
      cultural Economics* 27, No. 1(1976):1-16.

      Deals with a clash which arises out of the British
      twentieth century emphasis on the planned improvement
      of poor urban living conditions together with the
      protection of rural areas from nonagricultural develop-
      ment. The extent of the clash has been intensified by
      the industrial nature of modern farming processes, with
      rapid changes in farm buildings, agricultural land-
      scapes, and in effluent and noise pollution.

393. William, R. D. "Farming Systems Research and Small
      Farm Development in Rural Communities of North
      Florida." *Rural Development Research and Education*
      3, No. 4 (Winter 1979-80):7-9.

Describes efforts by university personnel to implement research and extension programs involving small-scale or limited-resource vegetable growers in north Florida.

394. Williams, Anne S. "Leadership Patterns in the Declining Rural Community." *Journal of Community Development Society* 5, No. 2(1974):98-106.

Reviews the literature on leadership patterns in declining rural communities and offers two suggestions for improvement: leadership training and redefining the boundaries of rural organizational units (counties) into larger multicounty areas that could more efficiently provide administrative and public services.

395. Williams, Daniel G. "Regional Development as Determined by Alternative Regional Goals." *Growth and Change* 14, No. 3(1983):23-37.

Examines for a small, multicounty region the relationships among alternative regional growth goals and the differences in such characteristics as industry mix and increases in regional wage and gross regional product that these different growth goals imply. Three counties in northwestern Arkansas are studied.

396. Wills, I. R. "Changes in Rural Land Use and Part-Time Farming, Central Victoria, 1974 to 1978." *Review of Marketing and Agricultural Economics* 51, No. 2(1983): 109-30.

Reveals that successive surveys of 376 rural holdings near Melbourne in 1974-75 and 1978-79 revealed a substantial increase in part-time farming at the expense of full-time farming, but little change in overall land use and area farmed. Few of the part-time farms surveyed were profitable in the mid-1970s, but most farmers put their farming way of life ahead of financial considerations, and the blow was softened by capital gains on farm land and the tax deductibility of farm losses. Part-time farms were a little less productive than neighboring full-time farms, but there was little evidence that small part-time farms were neglected or badly managed.

397. Wills, I. R. "Part-Time Farming in Central Victoria."
      Review of Marketing and Agricultural Economics 46,
      No. 3(1978):196-219.

      Reports the results of a survey of part-time farmers
      in two shires close to Melbourne in 1974-75. The
      farmers were a very diverse group in terms of off-farm
      employment and income; few derived substantial income
      from farming and the majority indicated that they
      farmed for nonfinancial reasons. Part-time farming
      appeared to be a stable working and living arrangement,
      and part-time farms were about as productive as full-
      time farms in the same shire.

398. Wimberl[e]y [*sic*], Ronald C., comp. and ed. *Rural
      Sociology in the South: 1982.* Proceedings of the
      Rural Sociology Section of the Southern Association
      of Agricultural Scientists. Raleigh, North Carolina:
      North Carolina State University, Department of
      Sociology and Anthropology, 1982. 401 pp.

      Is designed to show the major thrusts southern
      sociology is bringing to bear upon rural and agricul-
      tural problems, i.e., the sociology of agriculture, the
      sociology of communities, social change, social demog-
      raphy, the social problem of rural crime, human
      resources, and natural resources. Topics include rural
      sociology, land economics, management, production,
      statistical data and methodology, supply and demand,
      consumer economics, foreign development, regional and
      human development, and resource economics.

399. Winsberg, Morton D. "A Note on Locational Impacts in
      the South." *Growth and Change* 12, No. 3(1981):41-
      46.

      Assesses whether areas of the South have benefited
      from the construction of the interstate highway system
      by comparing 223 counties with an interstate highway
      with 558 counties without such a highway. Change in
      the value of farm sales was the primary variable
      examined. Over the period 1954-74 the interstate
      system appeared to have only minor effects on the
      location of agricultural production.

400. Young, Harold C., and R. H. Gibson. "Evaluating Agri-
      cultural Programs." *Growth and Change* 2, No.
      3(1971):42-46.

Illustrates a method of evaluating the Tributary Area Development program in the Elk River area of south central Tennessee. This agricultural program is discussed along with its impact on the Elk River area.

Federal Publications

Federal Publications

401. Banks, Vera J. *Farm Population Trends by Farm Characteristics, 1975-80.* Rural Dev. Res. Rpt. No. 40. Washington, D.C.: USDA, Economic Research Service, 1984. 40 pp. Doc. A93.41:40.

Presents estimates of the 1975 and 1980 farm populations by race, tenure status of operator, value of agricultural products sold, and type of farm. The study revealed that the number of persons living on larger farms jumped 67% during the time period while smaller and midsize farms together lost about 20% of their population. Smaller farms, however, still contained about half of the U.S. farm population, and larger farms accounted for only 18% of farm residents.

402. Banks, Vera J., and Judith Z. Kalbacher. *Farm Income Recipients and Their Families: A Socioeconomic Profile.* Rural Dev. Res. Rpt. No. 30. Washington, D.C.: USDA, Economic Research Service, 1981. 24 pp. Doc. A93.41:30.

Provides a detailed analysis of the socioeconomic and demographic characteristics of farm income recipients and their families. Recipients of farm self-employment income were more likely to be White, male, and older, and their families of the husband-wife type. Most were primarily employed in agriculture, but 44% indicated primary employment in nonagricultural industries. Data are based on a special tabulation of the March 1976 Current Population Survey.

403. Bender, Lloyd D., Bernal L. Green, Thomas F. Hady, John A. Kuehn, Marlys K. Nelson, Leon B. Perkinson, and Peggy J. Ross. *The Diverse Social and Economic Structure of Nonmetropolitan America.* Rural Dev. Res. Rpt. No. 49. Washington, D.C.: USDA, Economic Research Service, 1985. 28 pp. Doc. A93.41:49.

Identifies seven distinct types of rural counties
according to their major economic base, presence of
federally owned land, or population characteristics.
The types are farming dependent, manufacturing
dependent, mining dependent, government functions,
persistent poverty, federal lands, and retirement
settlements. Seven U.S. maps by county are included.

Compare with item 423.

404. Boxley, Robert F. "Farmland Ownership and the Distri-
      bution of Land Earnings." *Agricultural Economics
      Research* 37, No. 4 (1985):40-44. Washington, D.C.:
      USDA, Economic Research Service, Government Printing
      Office.

      Examines changes in U.S. farmland ownership and
      tenure over this century, analyzes differences in the
      distribution of farm operators and owners in 1979, and
      examines how land earnings may have been shared then.
      Boxley states that widespread agricultural landowner-
      ship by nonoperator landlords provides a mechanism for
      a substantial transfer of agricultural earnings and
      wealth away from farm operators and, potentially, away
      from the farm sector.

405. Brooks, Nora L. *Minifarms: Farm Business or Rural
      Residence.* Agr. Info. Bull. No. 480. Washington,
      D.C.: USDA, Economic Research Service, 1985. 17 pp.
      Doc. Al.75:480/2.

      Reports that minifarms (those with less than $2,500
      in farm sales annually) account for about 25 percent of
      all U.S. farms, almost 2 percent of U.S. harvested
      cropland, and less than 1 percent of U.S. farm product
      sales. Most minifarm operators spend over 200 days a
      year doing off-farm work. More than 54 percent of all
      minifarms are in the South, representing one-third of
      all farms in that region.

406. Brown, David L. "Farm Structure and the Rural
      Community." *Structure Issues of American Agriculture*
      (item 448), pp. 283-87. Doc. Al.107:438.

      Examines the effects on small towns of changes in
      transportation and communication and of structural
      changes in agriculture. More efficient transportation
      and communication have led to the specialization of

small towns. Structural changes not only cause small
towns to be less viable centers of farm inputs and
marketing but also cause businesses and institutions to
merge or consolidate.

407. Brown, David L., and Jeanne M. O'Leary. *Labor Force
Activity of Women in Metropolitan and Nonmetropolitan
America.* Rural Dev. Res. Rpt. No. 15. Washington,
D.C.: USDA, Economics, Statistics, and Cooperatives
Service, 1979. 33 pp. Doc. A93.41:15.

Describes trends and changes in women's employment
and labor force participation in metropolitan and
nonmetropolitan areas. Metro women are more likely to
be in the labor force than are nonmetro women, but the
difference in women's labor force participation rates
narrowed between 1960 and 1970. Women have become a
particularly important labor resource in nonmetro
counties, where they accounted for 89% of job growth
between 1960 and 1970. While not constrained to traditional rural pursuits, nonmetro women are more likely
to hold relatively low-wage clerical, operative, and
service jobs than their metro counterparts.

408. Chicoine, David L., and Norman Walzer. *Financing Rural
Roads and Bridges in the Midwest.* Washington, D.C.:
USDA, Office of Transportation and Agricultural
Marketing Services, October 1984. 225 pp. Doc.
HE356.A14C551984.

Examines the condition of rural roads and bridges in
four midwestern states: Illinois, Minnesota, Ohio, and
Wisconsin. Data collected from a mail survey of
farmers, township highway personnel, and agribusiness
users of rural transportation systems were examined in
the context of the financial resources available to
maintain or upgrade the facilities and in the context
of management practices followed in providing the
services.

See also item 469.

409. Congressional Research Service. *Agricultural Communities: The Interrelationship of Agriculture, Business, Industry, and Government in the Rural Economy:
A Symposium.* Prepared for the Committee on Agriculture, U.S. House of Representatives. Washington,
D.C.: Government Printing Office, 1983. 354 pp.

Summarizes a symposium held at the Library of Congress in May 1983. Seventeen papers are included, dealing with such topics as effects of agricultural structure on community development, credit institutions in agricultural communities, and the changing structure of local governments.

410. Daberkow, Stan G., and Herman Bluestone. *Patterns of Change in the Metro and Nonmetro Labor Force, 1976-82.* Rural Dev. Res. Rpt. No. 44. Washington, D.C.: USDA, Economic Research Service, 1984. 23 pp. Doc. A93.41:44.

Uses selected labor force indicators (employment, labor force, and the unemployment rate) to measure the economic performance of regions as well as metro, nonmetro, and farm areas for the period 1976-82. Results indicate that nonmetro areas, particularly farm areas, lagged behind metro areas in employment growth, especially in the South and West.

411. Daberkow, Stan G., Donald K. Larson, Robert Coltrane, and Thomas A. Carlin. *Distribution of Employment Growth in Nine Kentucky Counties.* Rural Dev. Res. Rpt. No. 41. Washington, D.C.: USDA, Economic Research Service, 1984. 35 pp. Doc. A93.41:41.

Is a case study that examines the distributional effects of rapid employment growth in a nonmetropolitan area. The location is a nine-county area of south central Kentucky. The study revealed that recent immigrants held a disproportionate share of better-paying executive and professional jobs and that they also held a disproportionate share of jobs in growing business establishments.

412. Davis, Thomas F. *Persistent Low-Income Counties in Nonmetro America.* Rural Dev. Res. Rpt. No. 12. Washington, D.C.: USDA, Economics, Statistics, and Cooperatives Service, 1979. 23 pp. Doc. A93.41:12.

Identifies 298 nonmetro counties that had persistent low incomes during the 1950-70 period. The population, employment, and income characteristics of these counties for 1969-75 are analyzed, and factors contributing to improved incomes are examined.

See also item 424.

413. Deavers, Kenneth L., and David L. Brown. *Natural Resource Dependence, Rural Development, and Rural Poverty.* Rural Dev. Res. Rpt. No. 48. Washington, D.C.: USDA, Economic Research Service, 1985. 16 pp. Doc. A93.41:48.

Examines the influence of natural resource dependence on rural income levels and recent population growth. Because the analysis did not provide convincing evidence that a county's dependence on farming, mining, or federally owned land affected community income, the authors focused on persistently poor rural counties regardless of their natural resource dependence.

414. Economic Development Division. *Small-Farm Issues: Proceedings of the ESCS Small-Farm Workshop, May 1978.* ESCS-60. Washington, D.C.: USDA, Economics, Statistics, and Cooperatives Service, 1978. 73 pp. Doc. A105.25:60.

Summarizes discussions at a conference devoted to the situation and needs of operators of small farms (defined as those with gross sales less than $20,000). Participants viewed small farms as an important way of life in the United States. Whereas traditional research and assistance programs offered by universities and the USDA have focused on farms as commercial production units, workshop participants cited the need for a new focus on the farm family as a production, social, and income-producing unit.

Contains item 436.

415. Fratoe, Frank A. *The Educational Level of Farm Residents and Workers.* Rural Dev. Res. Rpt. No. 8. Washington, D.C.: USDA, Economics, Statistics, and Cooperatives Service, 1979. 24 pp. Doc. A93.41:8.

Examines educational characteristics of the farm-related population, including nonmetro farm residents and workers, by race and sex. Results indicate that members of this population generally lagged behind their nonfarm-related counterparts in all areas examined: number of school years completed, number of persons completing high school and college, functional literacy rates, participation in adult education, and labor force status.

416. Fratoe, Frank A. *Rural Education and Rural Labor Force in the Seventies.* Rural Dev. Res. Rpt. No. 5. Washington, D.C.:   USDA, Economics, Statistics, and Cooperatives Service, 1978. 38 pp. Doc. A93.41:5.

Explores the relationship between education and rural development, and in doing so, presents a broad overview of the rural education situation in the seventies. The results suggest that migration may be a confounding factor because many better-educated rural people move to urban areas.

417. Goebel, Karen P. "Family Resource Management Efforts in Assisting Farm Families." *Outlook '86: Proceedings* (item 446), pp. 289-91.

Reviews programming efforts in various states to help farm families handle the economic, social, and psychological conditions confronting them in the 1980s.

418. Green, Bernal L., and Thomas A. Carlin. *Agricultural Policy, Rural Counties, and Political Geography.* ERS Staff Rpt. No. AGES850429. Washington, D.C.: USDA, Economic Research Service, 1985.   8 pp.   Doc. A93.44:AGES850429.

Points out that counties that depend economically on farming and receive large amounts of federal commodity payments will receive the greatest, most direct impact of farm policy adjustments. More than 700 of the nation's 2,443 rural counties are still depending on farming for at least 20% of their income and employment. This study, considering these as "farming-dependent" counties, identifies their geographic location and socioeconomic characteristics. These counties have become concentrated in a relatively small number of congressional districts in the nation's midsection, limiting their political strength in Congress where farm policy is determined.

419. Guither, Harold D., J. Paxton Marshall, and Paul W. Barkley. "Policies and Programs to Ease the Transition of Resources Out of Agriculture." *The Farm Credit Crisis: Policy Options and Consequences* (item 445), pp. 47-52.

Presents adjustment strategies which financially distressed farmers and agricultural communities may consider as they respond to the reality of excess resources in agriculture. The authors conclude that many financially distressed farmers will find it necessary to leave their farms and pursue other careers. Educational and skill training programs could help ease their transition to nonfarm employment. If this transition occurs on a widespread basis, some agriculturally centered communities may find it necessary to seriously reevaluate their future.

420. Gulley, James L. *Beliefs and Values in American Farming.* ERS-558. Washington, D.C.: USDA, Economic Research Service, 1974. 74 pp. Doc. A93.21:558.

Considers how the existing beliefs and values about agriculture arose and how they may be adjusted to the present age. The Protestant ethic of the virtue of work, for example, and the influence of frontier psychology are reviewed. Freedom, independence, and the family farm still sway our thinking although they have a different context than in Jefferson's day.

421. Hefferan, Colien. "Economic Outlook for Families— 1986." *Outlook '86: Proceedings* (item 446), pp. 267-78.

Reviews the economic conditions and trends affecting both the income and expenditure sides of the family ledger, as well as indicators of the ability of families to balance the two. Financial management issues are examined in light of current economic conditions and the outlook for families.

422. Hines, Fred K. "Regional Impacts of Financial Stress in Farming." *Outlook '86: Proceedings* (item 446), pp. 460-71.

Briefly outlines major national and international trends which are major contributors to the current farm crisis, then identifies and discusses various regional and community factors which affect a region's or community's vulnerability to the current crisis in agriculture.

423. Hoppe, Robert A. *Agricultural Counties: Their Location, Farms and Economies.* ESS Staff Rpt. No. AGESS 810213. Washington, D.C.: USDA, Economics and Statistics Service, Economic Development Division,

1981. Available from NTIS. 48 pp. Doc.
A93.44:AGESS810213.

Traces the decline in areas dependent on farming
since 1950. Rural areas still agriculturally dependent
are identified, and the structure of agriculture there
is examined. Of the 684 agricultural counties in the
midseventies, 673 had been consistently agricultural
since 1950. These counties had a disproportionate
share of the nation's large farms and have become
increasingly concentrated in the West North Central
states. Over three-fourths of the operators reported
farming as their principal occupation. The author also
discusses the importance of agriculture to rural
economies.

Compare with item 403.

424. Hoppe, Robert A. *Economic Structure and Change in
     Persistently Low-Income Nonmetro Counties.* Rural
     Dev. Res. Rpt. No. 50. Washington, D.C.: USDA,
     Economic Research Service, 1985. 25 pp. Doc.
     A93.41:50.

Builds on an earlier study that identified 298
nonmetro counties that had low incomes in 1950, 1959,
and 1969, and examines what happened to those persistently low-income counties in the seventies. Hoppe
characterizes these counties and identifies factors
that caused some counties to lose their persistently
low-income status.

See also item 412.

425. Larson, Donald K., and Claudia K. White. *Will Employ-
     ment Growth Benefit All Households? A Case Study in
     Nine Nonmetro Kentucky Counties.* Rural Dev. Res.
     Rpt. No. 55. Washington, D.C.: USDA, Economic
     Research Service, 1986. 24 pp. Doc. A93.41:55.

Indicates that overall employment growth in a rural
area will probably not benefit all households or
residents in that area. In a nine-county area of south
central Kentucky, rapid employment growth between 1974
and 1979 did create new job opportunities; however,
only 18% of the households had members who took advantage of new jobs. The employment growth also did not

reduce the area's overall poverty level. Some population groups, such as households headed by women,
remained economically disadvantaged despite the area's
growth. Other groups, such as the elderly, maintained
their income status by relying on public and private
income transfer programs.

426. Leistritz, F. Larry, Arlen G. Leholm, Steve H. Murdock,
and Rita R. Hamm. "The Current Farm Financial
Situation: Impact on Farm Operators and Rural
Communities." *Outlook '86: Proceedings* (item 446),
pp. 484-95.

Presents the results of a study designed to identify
key characteristics of North Dakota farm operators and
their families and provides insights concerning (1)
adjustments likely to be faced by the affected farm
operators and their families and (2) impacts likely to
be experienced by agriculturally dependent communities.
Specific characteristics examined include financial
characteristics, such as levels of assets, debt, and
income; demographic characteristics, such as age,
marital status, family size, and education; and employment history and vocational skills and preferences.

427. Morrissey, Elizabeth S. *Characteristics of Poverty in
Nonmetro Counties.* Rural Dev. Res. Rpt. No. 52.
Washington, D.C.: Economic Research Service, 1985.
10 pp. Doc. A93.41:52.

Examines some of the demographic, socioeconomic, and
employment differences between rural areas with high
poverty rates and low poverty rates. The report
identifies the unique characteristics of nonmetro
counties with large proportions of persons living in
poverty.

428. Reeder, Richard J. *Rural Governments: Raising
Revenues and Feeling the Pressure.* Rural Dev. Res.
Rpt. No. 51. Washington, D.C.: USDA, Economic
Research Service, 1985. 32 pp. Doc. A93.41:51.

Assesses fiscal pressures on local governments by
looking at locally raised revenues (taxes and user
fees) as a percentage of local income. It identifies
those nonmetro areas most affected by such fiscal
pressures and measures this pressure by examining the
level of local government revenue effort in 1977 and

whether that level rose or fell from 1972 to 1977.
Reeder concludes that many rural areas whose income and
population declined have increased revenue efforts and
that the high cost of providing public services in
sparsely populated areas contributed substantially to
rural fiscal pressure.

429. Salamon, Sonya. "Changing Family Farms and Rural
      Community Relationships." *Readings in Rural America.*
      Edited by Ronald C. Wimberley. Washington, D.C.:
      Joint Economic Committee of the Congress of the
      United States, 1986. 15 pp.

      Examines effects of changes in the structure of agri-
      culture on social relationships in rural communities.

430. Salant, Priscilla. *Farm Households and the Off-Farm
      Sector: Results From Mississippi and Tennessee.*
      Agr. Econ. Res. Rpt. No. 143. USDA, Economic
      Research Service, Washington, D.C., in cooperation
      with the Agricultural Experiment Station, Dept. of
      Agr. Econ., Mississippi State University, Mississippi
      State, Mississippi, 1984. 38 pp.

      Describes off-farm employment and income among farm
      households in the Sand-Clay Hills region of northern
      Mississippi and southwestern Tennessee. Over half of
      all farm operators and two-fifths of other family
      members age sixteen and over worked off the farm in
      1980. Off-farm employment was highly associated with
      smaller farms and less labor-intensive enterprises.
      Nonfarm income contributed significantly to total
      household income and helped families to escape poverty
      and to continue farming.

431. Salant, Priscilla, and Robert D. Munoz. *Rural Indus-
      trialization and Its Impact on the Agricultural
      Community: A Review of the Literature.* ESS Staff
      Report No. AGESS810316. Washington, D.C.: USDA,
      Economics and Statistics Service, 1981. 14 pp. Doc.
      A93.44:AGESS810316.

      Examines literature concerning (1) the link between
      farm scale and community welfare, and (2) the economic
      interface between agriculture and rural industrializa-
      tion. Several farm region case studies conclude that
      employment and social services are more varied where
      smaller, family farms prevail, in other words, where

agriculture is less "industrial." Other studies, undertaken in rural areas where industry has located, indicate that part-time farmers may benefit from greater employment opportunities if their skill levels match industry's demands.

432. Schaub, James D. *The Nonmetro Labor Force in the Seventies.* Rural Dev. Res. Rpt. No. 33. Washington, D.C.: USDA, Economic Research Service, 1981. 23 pp. Doc. A93.41:33.

Reports that metro and nonmetro areas experienced similar employment growth rates between 1973 and 1979; however, nonmetro residents continued to have lower labor force participation rates. American women increased their labor force participation and employment, but nonmetro women gained less in percentage terms than metro women. In both metro and nonmetro areas, Black and other minority populations showed little improvement in their labor force participation rate, with White women accounting for four-fifths of nonmetro teen employment growth. Older residents in nonmetro areas had low unemployment rates and maintained a higher labor force participation rate than their metro counterparts.

433. Schaub, James D., and Victor J. Oliveira. *Distribution of Employment Growth in 10 Georgia Counties: A Case Study.* Rural Dev. Res. Rpt. No. 53. Washington, D.C.: USDA, Economic Research Service, 1985. 39 pp. Doc. A93.41:53.

Reports that rapid economic growth in a ten-county rural area in south Georgia during 1976-81 favored employment of whites, men, and immigrants. They earned higher average weekly salaries than blacks, women, and long-term residents. This study of growth in a mixed manufacturing- and agricultural-based economy flows from a research project on the impacts of economic expansion in nonmetro economies with different industrial bases. The Georgia area's job growth was greatest in the trade and services sectors.

434. Scholl, Kathleen L. "Economic Outlook for Farm Families: 1986." *Outlook '86: Proceedings* (item 446), pp. 279-88.

Outlines macroeconomic forces affecting the economic health of U.S. agriculture and the implications of those trends for farm families. Family financial management strategies appropriate for coping with difficult economic conditions are outlined.

435. Smith, Leslie Whitener, and Robert Coltrane. *Hired Farmworkers: Backgrounds and Trends for the Eighties*. Rural Dev. Res. Rpt. No. 32. Washington, D.C.: USDA, Economic Research Service, 1981. 31 pp. Doc. A93.41:32.

Examines historic and current trends in farm employment in the United States by focusing on the numbers and characteristics of hired farmworkers and migratory labor. Factors affecting the size and composition of the farm work force are identified, and probable farm employment trends in the eighties are examined.

436. Sonka, Steven T. "The Research Needs of Small Farmers." *Small-Farm Issues: Proceedings of the ESCS Small-Farm Workshop, May 1978* (item 414), pp. 31-36.

Points out that economic activity in rural communities is inversely related to average farm size. Less economic activity is generated in rural communities serving agriculture as farms grow larger and fewer people remain in the farming sector. Thus, as farmers adjust to pressures to expand and improve their economic well-being, they simultaneously tend to reduce the economic well-being of people in the rural communities surrounding them.

437. U.S. Congress, House. *Family Farm Development Act of 1980*. Hearings before the Subcommittee on Family Farms, Rural Development, and Special Studies on H.R. 6295. Washington, D.C.: Government Printing Office, 1980. 183 pp. Doc. Y4.Ag8/1:96-PPP.

Presents testimony of farmers, realtors, and administrators on H.R. 6295, a bill to encourage the ownership and development of family farms, to provide for research and education relating to family farms, to authorize the President to stabilize food prices, to authorize the Secretary of Agriculture to provide financial assistance for the production of industrial hydrocarbons and alcohols from agricultural commodities and forest products, and for other purposes.

438. U.S. Congress, House. *Obstacles to Strengthening Family Farm System.* Hearings before the Subcommittee on Family Farms, Rural Development, and Special Studies. Washington, D.C.: Government Printing Office, 1977. 736 pp. Doc. Y4.Ag8/1:F21/3.

Presents statements on obstacles to strengthening the family farm system with particular emphasis on competition for land and its implications for farm operators and community development efforts in small towns.

439. U.S. Congress, House. *Rural Community Development Act and Rural Development Policy Act.* Hearings before the Subcommittee on Family Farms, Rural Development, and Special Studies. Washington, D.C.: Government Printing Office, 1978. 593 pp. Doc. Y4.Ag8/1:R88/23.

Presents statements regarding H.R. 9983, a bill to establish a separate community development program for units of general local government which have a population of 20,000 or fewer and are located in nonmetropolitan areas, and regarding H.R. 10885, a bill to establish a council to assist in meeting the development needs of rural areas of the United States and for other purposes.

440. U.S. Congress, Office of Technology Assessment. *Technology, Public Policy, and the Changing Structure of American Agriculture.* OTA-F-284. Washington, D.C.: Government Printing Office, 1986. 374 pp. Doc. Y3.T22/2:2T22/17.

Addresses the long-run effects that technology and certain other factors will have on American agriculture during the remainder of this century. It focuses on the relationship of technology to agricultural production, structural change, rural communities, environment and natural resource base, finance and credit, research and extension, and public policy. The assessment identifies many benefits that new technologies will create, but these benefits will also exact substantial costs in potential adjustment problems.

This report is a step toward understanding these inter-
related problems and identifying policies to ameliorate
them.

441. U.S. Congress, Senate. *Farm Credit Problems and Their
Impact on Agricultural Banks.* Hearings before the
Subcommittee on Small Business: Family Farm.
Washington, D.C.: Government Printing Office, 1985.
218 pp. Doc. Y4.Sml/2:S.hrg.99-14.

Includes statements of senators and representatives
of the farm credit system on the credit problems in the
Farm Belt and the impacts they have on agricultural
lenders.

442. U.S. Congress, Senate. *Governing the Heartland: Can
Rural Communities Survive the Farm Crisis?* Prepared
by the Subcommittee on Intergovernmental Relations of
the Committee on Governmental Affairs. Washington,
D.C., May 1986 (draft). 56 pp.

Documents the problems of rural community officials
faced with a declining revenue base. The report
examines the agricultural economy of the eighties,
estimated property tax impacts in agriculturally dependent counties, local government expenditures and future
impacts on it, long-term effects on communities, and
policy options.

443. U.S. Congress, Senate. *Impact of the Payment-in-Kind
Program on Agricultural Support Industries.* Hearing
before the Subcommittee on Small Business: Family
Farm. Washington, D.C.: Government Printing Office,
1983. 125 pp. Doc. Y4.Sml/2:S.hrg.98-348.

Presents statements by senators, government
officials, and agribusinessmen on the impact of the
Payment-in-Kind (PIK) program on agricultural support
industries.

444. U.S. Congress, Senate. *The Issue of Corporate Buyouts
of Family Farms.* Hearing before the Subcommittee on
Small Business: Family Farm. Washington, D.C.:
Government Printing Office, 1984. 210 pp. Doc.
Y4.Sml/2:S.hrg.98-969.

Includes statements by senators, government officials, and representatives of farmers' organizations on the topic of corporate buyouts of family farms.

445. U.S. Department of Agriculture. *The Farm Credit Crisis: Policy Options and Consequences.* Washington, D.C.: USDA, Extension Service, in cooperation with the Farm Foundation, Oak Brook, Illinois, 1986. 57 pp.

Contains eight articles documenting the broad spectrum of policy options available to deal with the farm credit crisis. Emphasis is placed upon a description of options and their consequences for farm operators, agricultural lenders, and rural communities as well as for the national supply-demand balance for farm commodities and governmental costs.

Contains item 419.

446. U.S. Department of Agriculture. *Outlook '86: Proceedings.* Washington, D.C.: USDA, Agricultural Outlook Conference, 1986. 546 pp.

Contains the proceedings of the USDA's 62d annual agricultural outlook conference. Topics include the farm economy, major commodities, rural Americans, food and nutrition, policy, financial conditions in the farm sector, and biotechnology.

Contains items 417, 421, 422, 426, 434.

447. U.S. Department of Agriculture. *Rural Development and the American Farm: A Partnership for Progress.* (Cover title reads *Rural Communities and the American Farm.*) Washington, D.C.: USDA, Office of Rural Development Policy, 1984. 30 pp. Doc. A102.2:R88.

Sets forth the rural development policy statement presented to Congress in 1984 by the Office of Rural Development Policy. The office found that over a million farm families depend on off-farm sources for a large portion of their annual income and that most of that off-farm income is derived from other rural enterprises. Thus, the very economic survival of these farm families depends heavily on the vitality of the nonfarm rural economy.

448. U.S. Department of Agriculture. *Structure Issues of American Agriculture*. Agr. Econ. Rpt. 438. Washington, D.C.: USDA, Economics, Statistics, and Cooperatives Service, 1979. 300 pp. Doc. Al.107:438.

Includes discussions on the changing economy and structure of agriculture, farm production (land values, tenure, economies of size, technology, credit, labor, and entry and exit barriers and incentives), public policies (taxation, land and water use, price and income policies, environmental regulations, energy, and transportation), marketing (inputs industry, retailing, cooperatives, international markets, and food policy), rural America (off-farm employment, small farms, rural communities) and the experiences of other countries.

449. U.S. General Accounting Office. *Changing Character and Structure of American Agriculture: An Overview*. CED-78-178. Washington, D.C.: Government Printing Office, September 1978. 160 pp. Doc. GA1.13:CED-78-178.

Discusses the importance of agriculture and its changing character and structure and presents a series of major policy issues. Among the topics discussed are agriculture's role in the economy; narrowing profit margins; increased mechanization and capital requirements; government programs; and farm size, income, and ownership.

450. Wimberl[e]y [*sic*], Ronald C., and Charles N. Bebee. *Structure of U.S. Agriculture Bibliography*. Bibliographies and Literature of Agriculture No. 16. Washington, D.C.: USDA, Science and Education Administration, [1981]. 514 pp. Doc. Al.60/3:16.

Offers references to various scientific and policy materials on the structure of agriculture. The bibliography was extracted from the Agriculture On-Line Access (AGRICOLA) family of data bases for the years 1970-1979. Topics include rural sociology, land economics, management, production, statistical data and methodology, supply and demand, consumer economics, foreign development, regional and human development, and resource economics.

Other Research Reports

Other Research Reports

451. American Agricultural Economics Association. *Agriculture and Rural Areas Approaching the Twenty-first Century: Challenges for Agricultural Economics.* Conference papers. Oak Brook, Illinois: Farm Foundation, 1985. 291 pp.

Includes papers presented at an agricultural economics conference that sought to redefine agricultural issues by (1) characterizing the changing state of agriculture and the rural community; (2) assaying the changing state of economic logic and quantitative methods; (3) exploring how the analysis of problems of agriculture and the rural community can make a contribution to improvements in logic, data, and methods; and (4) identifying and defining significant problems of agriculture and the rural community and the issues needing attention by agricultural economics research, teaching, and extension.

452. Anderson, A. H. *The "Expanding" Rural Community.* Bull. 464. Lincoln, Nebraska: Agricultural Experiment Station, University of Nebraska, 1961.

Reports findings from a study of six counties in Nebraska's transition zone between the humid east and semiarid west. Community change resulting from agricultural adjustment to factors, such as decline in farm population and development of large service areas, is examined.

453. Anderson, A. H., and C. J. Miller. *The Changing Role of the Small Town in Farm Areas.* Bull. 419. Lincoln, Nebraska: Agricultural Experiment Station, University of Nebraska, 1953.

Presents a case study of a small rural Nebraska town of 500 population. Examined were the range of business services and farm trade, farm markets, institutional

and social center changes, age of population, urbanization of rural areas, and the organization of the
community.

454. Anderson, Dale G., Floyd D. Gaibler, and Mary Berglund.
*Economic Impact of Railroad Branch-line Abandonments:
Results of a Southcentral Nebraska Case Study.*
SB541.   Lincoln, Nebraska: University of Nebraska,
1976. 26 pp.

Assesses the impact of branch-line abandonment on
country elevators and surrounding communities. A model
was used to evaluate the economic feasibility of alternative   grain-handling   systems   given   existing and
prospective   freight   rates   for   alternative   transport
modes, elevator costs for various sizes of facilities,
and grain prices at alternative destinations.

455. Barkley, Paul W.   *Area Development: The Changing Role
of Some Communities in South-Central Kansas.*
Manhattan, Kansas: Cooperative Extension   Service,
Kansas State University, 1962.

Analyzes historical developments and population characteristics of Rice County, Kansas.   Barkley concludes
that   small   rural   communities   will   serve   primarily as
places of residence in the future and that the county's
larger   communities   will   face   considerable   competition
from larger communities of surrounding counties.

456. Barkley, Paul W., and Joanne Buteau.   *The Economics of
Rural Businessmen: A Case Study in Lincoln County,
Washington.* WRDC Discussion Paper No. 3. Corvallis,
Oregon: Western Rural Development Center, 1974.   22
pp.

Reports   preliminary   findings   from a study   of forty-
three businessmen located in several small agricultural
trade centers in east central Washington.   Results suggest   that   while   some   business   opportunity   remains in
these   towns,   the   capital   values   of   most   businesses'
assets are declining, their clientele groups are becom-
ing   smaller,   and   they   feel   increased   pressure   from
government   regulations,   cooperative   stores,   and   tax-
exempt   properties   in   their   towns.   Their   adaptive
strategies vary by size of place, type of business, and
age of operator.

457. Barrows, Richard, Ed Jesse, Bruce Jones, Rick Klemme, Glen Pulver, and William Saupe. *Financial Status of Wisconsin Farming, 1986.* Madison, Wisconsin: University of Wisconsin Cooperative Extension Service, 1986. 42 pp.

Documents the nature of farm financial stress in Wisconsin and examines the consequences of alternative policy responses for farm families and rural communities. The extent to which farm financial failures will affect rural communities is expected to depend on the extent of the area's economic dependence on agriculture.

458. Bartruff, Stuart, Ron Hanson, and Bruce Johnson. "Nebraska Firms Like to Hire Farmers." *Farm, Ranch, and Home Quarterly.* Lincoln, Nebraska: University of Nebraska, Winter 1979. pp. 11-13.

Summarizes results of a survey of twenty-one manufacturing firms in eastern Nebraska. The manufacturers' attitudes toward farm family employees, as compared to nonfarm employees, were examined.

459. Bauder, Ward W. *The Impact of Population Change on Rural Community Life: The Economic System.* Ames, Iowa: Iowa State University, November 1962.

Examines the shifting of trade areas within Greene County, Iowa, from 1900 to 1960 and the adjustments that trade centers made to a declining and aging population.

460. Bertrand, Alvin L., and Harold W. Osborne. *Rural Industrialization in a Louisiana Community.* Bull. No. 524. Baton Rouge, Louisiana: Louisiana State University, 1959, in cooperation with USDA, Agricultural Economics Division, Farm Population and Rural Life Branch. 39 pp.

Presents results of a study to determine the impacts of industry in rural areas. Answers to the following questions were sought: Whom does a rural industry employ? How does rural industry affect the economic and social well-being of a community, its social institutions, and the agricultural practices in a community? What are the attitudes of rural people toward industrial employment?

461. Bollman, Ray D. *Off Farm Work by Farmers.* Census
     Analytical Study. Catalogue 99-756E. Ottawa,
     Ontario, Canada: Minister of Supply and Services,
     Statistics Canada, 1979. 214 pp.

     Provides a broad analysis of social and economic
     phenomena in Canada. Specific sections of the report
     discuss the theory of off-farm work and probability
     response models, the history of part-time farming in
     Canada, the development of an estimating equation, the
     contribution of part-time farmers to agricultural
     production, and the contribution of off-farm employment
     to the total income of farmers. An extensive bibliog-
     raphy on part-time farming is included.

462. Boody, George, and Michael Rivard. *Economic and Social
     Vulnerability in Rural Minnesota: An Urgent Needs
     and Resource Assessment.* Final Report to the Rural
     Strategy Task Force. Minneapolis: The Rural Enter-
     prise Institute, 1986. 35 pp. plus appendixes.

     Tracks the impacts of the farm crisis in rural Minne-
     sota and identifies additional negative economic forces
     which may worsen the crisis. The concept of vulnera-
     bility is used to tie together dynamics of economic
     shock, social suffering, cummulative emotional
     distress, and population displacement. Central to the
     discussion are the structural changes taking place in
     farming and the rural economy.

463. Broussard, Kathryn A., and Arthur M. Heagler. *An
     Economic Analysis of the Impact Associated With the
     Employment of Farm Women in the Farm Labor Force.*
     D.A.E. Res. Rpt. No. 650. Baton Rouge, Louisiana:
     Agricultural Experiment Station, Louisiana State
     University, 1986. 56 pp.

     Presents the results of a study designed to evaluate
     the economic impact associated with the employment of
     farm women in the farm labor force. Interviews were
     conducted with farm women on rice and soybean farms in
     Jefferson Davis Parish to obtain the data used in
     estimating the female farm labor resource. The oppor-
     tunity costs associated with employment either on or
     off the farm were estimated.

464. Brown, James S. "Programs Related to Family and
     Community Adjustments as Affected by Mobility Needs."

Labor Mobility and Population in Agriculture (item 502), pp. 213-19.

Contends that each region must prepare its people for participation in a national society, but in ways appropriate to the region; that policy must be oriented to full development of human potentialities; that the metropolitan region should be a major unit for research and policy; that programs for the southern Appalachian region need to help the population prepare for efficient migration; and that programs are needed to enable the family and community to adjust to agricultural changes.

465. Buttel, Frederick H., Mark Lancelle, and David R. Lee. *Emerging Agricultural Technologies, Farm Structural Change, Public Policy, and Rural Communities in the Northeast.* A.E. Res. 85-17. Ithaca, New York: Cornell University, 1985. 99 pp.

Reviews the historical and contemporary literature on the relationship between technological, farm structural, and rural community change in the Northeast region. The overall objective is to increase understanding of how emergent agricultural technologies will affect farm structure and rural communities over the next two decades.

466. Buzenberg, Mildred E. *The Interrelationships of Region, Population Change, and Change in Number of Retail Firms in Selected Areas of Nonmetropolitan Kansas.* Bull. No. 2. Manhattan, Kansas: Agricultural Experiment Station, Kansas State University, 1963.

Examines the relationship between population change in selected Kansas towns of less than 2,500 population and the composition of retail stores.

467. Carlin, Thomas A., and David Houston. "Small Farm Policy: What Role For the Government." *Increasing Understanding of Public Problems and Policies--1981.* Oak Brook, Illinois: Farm Foundation, 1981. pp. 30-40.

Generalizes small farm concerns into two broad schools. The first, and older of the two, is concerned primarily with the disadvantaged conditions faced by

some farmers unable to increase returns from their
farms or increase income through off-farm employment
and with policies to improve their well-being. The
second school emerged during the late 1960s and 1970s
and focuses on the industrialization of agriculture,
i.e., the increasing concentration of farm production
among fewer businesses. This school is concerned about
government policies which foster the further industrialization of farming, and advocates changes which might
enhance the competitive position of medium- and
smaller-sized farm businesses.

468.   Chicoine, David L. "Infrastructure and Agriculture:
       Interdependencies with a Focus on Local Roads in the
       North Central States." *Interdependencies of Agricul-
       ture and Rural Communities in the Twenty-first
       Century: The North Central Region* (item 514), pp.
       141-63.

       Presents a systematic approach to the relationship
       between agriculture and the rural road infrastructure.
       The paper includes a brief conceptual discussion, a
       review of national infrastructure concerns, a histori-
       cal discussion and institutional arrangements for
       meeting rural road service demands, evidence on demand
       for local rural road services, the current status of
       the road system, and road expenditures and financing in
       the North Central states.

469.   Chicoine, David L., and Norman Walzer. *Illinois Town-
       ship Roads and Bridges: Conditions, Demands, and
       Financing.* AE 4596. Urbana-Champaign, Illinois:
       University of Illinois, 1985. 43 pp.

       Focuses on rural roads and bridges, an important seg-
       ment of the infrastructure maintained by local govern-
       ments in Illinois. The condition, the service demands,
       and the financing of the system of rural roads and
       bridges under the jurisdiction of road districts are
       identified in some detail. The condition of the system
       is described using perceptions of responsible local
       officials and the main users of the system—Illinois
       farmers and agribusiness. Indications of farm and
       agribusiness service demand and information on funding
       levels are presented.

       See also item 408.

470. Chittick, Douglas. *Growth and Decline of South Dakota Trade Centers 1901-51.* Bulletin 448. Brookings, South Dakota: South Dakota State University, 1955. 55 pp.

Attempts to find a pattern in the complex changes that have taken place in the trade centers and farm areas of South Dakota from 1901 to 1951. The report closes with a discussion of the factors related to trends of growth and decline in trade centers.

471. Christiansen, John R., Sheridan Maitland, and John W. Payne. *Industrialization and Rural Life in Two Central Utah Counties.* Bull. 416. Logan, Utah: Agricultural Experiment Station, Utah State University, [1960]. 32 pp.

Presents results of a 1958 survey to appraise some of the social and economic changes which occurred in the lives of rural residents when an industrial plant was established in their community. Farm and nonfarm workers at the plant were compared. One fourth of the plant workers were farmers who used more hired labor and generally raised crops or livestock requiring less labor than did full-time farmers in the survey.

472. Cohen, Lois K., and G. Edward Schuh. *Job Mobility and Migration in a Middle Income Small Town with Comparisons to High and Low Income Communities.* Res. Bull. No. 763. Lafayette, Indiana: Purdue University Agricultural Experiment Station, 1963. 22 pp.

Examines the relationship between job mobility and migration in three Indiana communities. Job mobility refers to a change in type of employment; migration refers to movement from one community to another. Dual mobility involves both types of changes. The authors found that job mobility is greater for younger workers and for those with greater job skills and job knowledge.

473. Conklin, Neilson D., Richard M. Adams, and Carl E. Olson. *Labor Market Adjustments and Wyoming Agriculture: Some Effects on a Hypothetical East Central Wyoming Cattle Ranch.* RJ 134. Laramie, Wyoming: Agricultural Experiment Station, University of Wyoming, 1979. 24 pp.

Investigates the transfer of labor between the mining and agricultural sectors in Wyoming. Specifically analyzed were the effects of changing wage rates and labor availability on a hypothetical cattle ranch, as measured by changes in returns to the operator's labor, management and capital, and adjustments in the ranch's resource use.

474. Cortez, Isabelita V., and George R. Winter. *Part Time Farming in the Lower Fraser Valley of British Columbia.* Vancouver, British Columbia: University of British Columbia, Department of Agricultural Economics, November 1974. 97 pp.

Describes a study of the social and economic characteristics of part-time farmers in British Columbia. The analysis identifies the characteristics of part-time farmers, the factors influencing the extent of part-time farming, the productivity of part-time farmers, their land use and labor efficiency, the quality of their farm produce, their permanent or transitory status, and their contribution to the economy of British Columbia.

475. Council for Agricultural Science and Technology (CAST). *Agricultural Mechanization: Physical and Societal Effects and Implications for Policy Development.* Rpt. No. 96. Ames, Iowa: Council for Agricultural Science and Technology, 1983. 27 pp.

Addresses the effects of agricultural mechanization upon the American farm, the rural community, and society in general. The authors point out that the decrease in agricultural employment over the years has affected many agricultural communities. Most of the outmigration occurred among young people just entering the labor force. The eventual consequences of this depopulation include closing and consolidation of schools, decline in community morale, closing of small-town businesses, abandonment of country churches, withering of social organizations, inactivity of community and civic organizations, and a decline in relative value of property in affected communities.

476. Crecink, John C. *Small Farms: Their Distribution, Characteristics, and Households.* Agr. Econ. Res. Rpt. 161. Mississippi State, Mississippi:

Mississippi Agriculture and Forestry Experiment
Station, 1986. 36 pp.

Reports that, depending upon the definition, between
53% and 71% of U.S. farms in 1980 were classified as
small. Two geographic regions, the North Central and
the South, had about 84% of the nation's small farms.
Two distinct types of small, low-income farms were
identified: the "hard core" and the "transitory." The
"hard core" were those where households received net
money incomes below the nonmetropolitan median household income and also had farm sales of less than
$20,000. Most of the transitory small farms, with farm
household income below the nonmetropolitan median but
with farm sales of $20,000 or more, were found in the
North Central region. Various characteristics of these
two types of small farms and their operators are
examined.

477. Darling, David L., and Robert Sampson. *Assessing the
Role of Agriculture in a County's Economy.* EC-475.
West Lafayette, Indiana: Purdue University, Coopera-
tive Extension Service, 1978. 7 pp.

Describes a procedure for assessing the role of agriculture's income contribution to a county's economy.
Data for Clay County, Indiana, were used in the
example.

478. Desmarais, Ralph, and Edd Jeffords, eds. *Uncertain
Harvest: The Family Farm in Arkansas.* Eureka
Springs, Arkansas: Ozark Institute, 1980. 140 pp.

Focuses on the problems in rural Arkansas, particularly those of small farmers, and presents statements
of persons involved with these problems--farmers,
academicians, politicians, citizens. Also included is
a section on the interdependencies between (1) problems
on small farms and (2) changes in agribusiness activity
and on large farms.

479. Eldridge, Eber. "Trends Related to Rural Areas."
*Papers of the Rural Community Development Seminar:
Focus on Iowa.* Rural Development Special Series.
Ames, Iowa: Iowa State University, Center for Agri-
cultural and Rural Development, 1972. Section B.

Discusses the following trends in rural areas: those related to agricultural production, total employment in Iowa, retailing, institutions (churches, schools, and local government), health care, population, and income. Eldridge defines rural areas as any community and its surrounding area that depends substantially upon agriculture for its economic reason for existence.

480. Findeis, Jill L.   *The Importance of Off-Farm Income to Agriculture.* Staff Paper No. 112.   University Park, Pennsylvania: Pennsylvania State University, Department of Agricultural Economics and Rural Sociology, 1986.   11 pp.

Examines the implications of off-farm income from the standpoint of the future of agriculture in Pennsylvania and in the broader context of the state's rural economic development.   Findeis examines the prevalence of off-farm income, factors affecting the willingness and ability to work off the farm, and the relationship between agriculture and the rural economy.

481. Fisher, Peter S.   *The Impact of Rural Non-Farm Residential Development on the Provision of Local Public Services.*   Iowa City, Iowa: Institute of Urban and Regional Research, University of Iowa, 1979.   55 pp.

Provides a preliminary assessment of the impacts of rural nonfarm development in Iowa on the provision of public services by counties, special districts, and homeowners' associations.

482. Fitzgerald, Kath, Bob Hall, and David Thorns.   *Locality Studies: A Bibliography and Index.*   Working Paper No. 5.   Christchurch, New Zealand: University of Canterbury, Department of Sociology, October 1983. 147 pp.

Lists nearly 1,500 English-language references on the topic of social relationships within a locality. Included are urban, suburban, and rural materials as well as works relating to the historical reconstruction of localities.

483. Fliegel, Frederick C., J. C. van Es, Rabel J. Burdge, and Harvey J. Schweitzer.   *Farming in an Urban*

Environment. AERR 167. Urbana, Illinois: Agricultural Experiment Station, University of Illinois, Department of Agricultural Economics, 1979. 29 pp.

Presents results of a survey of 8,000 Illinois farm, nonfarm, and urban residents on the topics of land use, regulatory programs, and local community issues. Results indicate that the traditional contrasts between farmer and urbanite have become blurred and that the arena for decision making is increasingly the larger society.

484. Food and Agriculture Organization of the United Nations. *Women and Family in Rural Development: Annotated Bibliography.* Rome, Italy: Food and Agricultural Organization (FAO) of the United Nations, 1977. 60 pp.

Organizes FAO documents related to population, agricultural, and food issues into a bibliography on women and rural development for the years 1967 to 1977. Documents are identified by year, author, topic, and language. Most reports relate to developing countries and are in English.

485. Fuguitt, Glenn, Anthony Fuller, Heather Fuller, Ruth Gasson, and Gwyn Jones. *Part-time Farming: Its Nature and Implications.* Ashford, Kent, England: Wye College (University of London), Centre for European Agricultural Studies, 1977. 42 pp.

Defines part-time farming and discusses its implications for agricultural policy and its role in rural development and regional planning.

486. Fuller, Varden. *Rural Worker Adjustment to Urban Life: An Assessment of the Research.* Policy Papers in Human Resources and Industrial Relations 15. Ann Arbor, Michigan: University of Michigan, Institute of Labor and Industrial Relations, 1970. 87 pp.

Investigates how well the rural labor force has adjusted to the urban setting. Fuller examines agricultural technological advance, opportunities and uncertainties in the economic environment for off-farm migrants, attributes and influences in mobility, differential mobility by ethnic groups and regions, and attributes and influences in assimilation.

487. Galpin, C. J.   *The Social Anatomy of an Agricultural Community*. Madison, Wisconsin: Agricultural Experiment Station, University of Wisconsin, 1915.   Reproduced in 1969. 34 pp.

Studies the interrelationships between the farmer and the townsman in Walworth County, Wisconsin, in an attempt to cast light on the then-current rural problems of education, local government, and religion.

488. Gasson, Ruth, ed.   *The Place of Part-time Farming in Rural and Regional Development*. Proceedings of a seminar held at Wye College, 11-14 July 1977. Ashford, Kent, England: Wye College, 1977. 145 pp.

Collects eight papers on the implications of part-time farming for the rural-urban fringe, for less-favored areas, for income and price policy, and for the collection and interpretation of statistics.

Contains item 504.

489. Goldsmith, Harold E.   *Metropolitan Dominance and Agriculture in the Northeast*.   University Park, Pennsylvania: Pennsylvania State University, Department of Agricultural Economics and Rural Sociology, January 1963.

Examines the dominance or structuring influence cities have upon agriculture. Four aspects of dominance are examined: the influence of large urban centers upon the hinterlands, the influence of location within the inner or outer zone of metropolitan areas, the influence of the major metropolitans, and the influence of size of the urban place (especially those places not yet labeled as metropolitan).

490. Goreham, Gary A., F. Larry Leistritz, and Richard W. Rathge.   *Trade and Marketing Patterns of North Dakota Farm and Ranch Operators*. Agr. Econ. Misc. Rpt. No. 98.   Fargo, North Dakota: Agricultural Experiment Station, North Dakota State University, 1986. 40 pp.

Examines the trade and marketing patterns of North Dakota farm and ranch operators. Little support was found for the Goldschmidt thesis which suggests that trade patterns differ by size of agricultural operation. The results were similar to those of Korsching in his study of Iowa farmers.

See also items 54 and 76.

491. Great Plains Agricultural Council. *Energy Related Impacts on Great Plains Agricultural Productivity in the Next Quarter Century 1976-2000.* GPAC Pub. No. 82. Lincoln, Nebraska: Agricultural Experiment Station, University of Nebraska, 1976. 26 pp.

Addresses the anticipated impacts of energy-related problems on the agricultural and associated enterprises of the Great Plains. Energy development in certain areas will impose major stresses on land use, water, capital, labor, and community services development and will impact agriculture locally.

492. Hamilton, J. R., D. V. Peterson, and R. Reid. *Small Towns in a Rural Area: A Study of the Problems of Small Towns in Idaho.* Res. Bull. No. 91. Moscow, Idaho: Agricultural Experiment Station, University of Idaho, 1976. 126 pp.

Focuses on rural small towns and small town businesses to isolate and examine some of the economic forces which pressure community residents and merchants to ultimately shape and reshape their towns. Six towns were studied.

493. Hanson, R. J., and R. G. F. Spitze. *An Economic Analysis of Off-Farm Income in the Improvement of Illinois Farm Family Income.* AERR 139. Urbana-Champaign, Illinois: University of Illinois, Department of Agricultural Economics, 1976. 43 pp.

Estimates the flow of farm and off-farm income to Illinois farm families, analyzes the relationship between off-farm earnings and various farm and operator characteristics, and assesses the implications of off-farm income for rural development programs. Data for the analysis were obtained from 1,400 Illinois farmers for the year 1971.

494. Heady, Earl O., and Steven T. Sonka. *Farm-Size Structure and Off-Farm Income and Employment Generation in the North Central Region.* Ames, Iowa: North Central Regional Center for Rural Development, 1975. 91 pp.

Investigates how size of farm is related to the
welfare of both farm and nonfarm segments of society.
Specifically, the study relates farm-size structure to
total income in the farm sector, the number and size of
farms, income per farm, secondary income generation,
and consumer food costs. Impacts of differing farm
sizes on the North Central region are emphasized. To
examine the effect of differing farm sizes, alternative
farm structures are developed which specify that only a
certain size of farm may exist under each. Outcomes
under these different situations are then compared to
provide quantitative indications of farm-size effects
nationally and in the North Central region.

495. Healy, Robert G., and James L. Short. *The Market for*
      Rural Land: Trends, Issues, Policies. Washington,
      D.C.: Conservation Foundation, 1981.

      Defines rural land and rural land-market trends,
      describes the supply and demand for rural lands and how
      the land market functions, and concludes with an analy-
      sis of six case studies of the rural land market in
      Virginia, Texas, West Virginia, Illinois, New
      Hampshire, and California.

496. Heffernan, William D. "Agricultural Structure and the
      Community." *Can the Family Farm Survive?* (item
      550), 77 pp.

      Presents some results of a comparison of community
      life of family farmers and of farmers involved in
      contract broiler production with that of workers and
      managers of larger-than-family farms in north central
      Louisiana. The author discusses the importance of
      community life and concludes that the family farmers
      are associated with higher levels of community involve-
      ment than are corporate farmhands.

497. Heffernan, William D., and Rex R. Campbell. "Agricul-
      ture and the Community: The Sociological
      Perspective." *Interdependencies of Agriculture and*
      Rural Communities in the Twenty-first Century: The
      North Central Region (item 514), pp. 41-54.

      Briefly reviews the literature on the topic from a
      sociological viewpoint, then focuses on the changing
      sources of income and employment in rural communities.
      Possible community types of the future are suggested.

498. Hines, Fred, Mindy Petrulis, and Stan Daberkow. "An Overview of the Nonmetro Economy and the Role of Agriculture in Nonmetro Development." *Interdependencies of Agriculture and Rural Communities in the Twenty-first Century: The North Central Region* (item 514), pp. 15-40.

Presents a historical and current overview of the economic conditions in metropolitan and nonmetropolitan America and provides insights into the role agriculture plays in nonmetro development. The focus is on Midwestern states.

499. Hoiberg, Eric O., and Paul Lasley. "Part-time and Limited Resource Farms and Economic and Social Growth in Rural Areas." *Interdependencies of Agriculture and Rural Communities in the Twenty-first Century: The North Central Region* (item 514), pp. 93-107.

Analyzes the relationship between limited resource and part-time farming and the process of development in rural areas. A farm typology is formulated, and benefits of small and part-time farming to the community are discussed along with impacts of the community on farming.

500. Hoover, Herbert, and John C. Crecink. *Part-time Farming: Its Role and Prospects in the Clay-Hill Area of Mississippi.* No. 627. Mississippi State, Mississippi: Mississippi State University, 1961. 21 pp.

Investigates the role of part-time farming and the prospects of the part-time farm group in the agricultural economy of the area. Investigated were family and farm characteristics, levels of income, off-farm employment opportunities, farm production and efficiency, and part-time farming as a transitional phase.

501. House, Verne W., Kane C. Quenemoen, and Anne Hill. *Alternative Methods of Maintaining Land in Agriculture.* Bull. 1262. Bozeman, Montana: Montana State University, Cooperative Extension Service, revised 1983. 41 pp.

Reviews alternative policies and programs designed to assure the retention of farm and other open space land.

Topics discussed include differential assessment, tax issues, zoning, development rights, land banking, conservation easements, agricultural districts, and farmland transfer fee plans. Wisconsin's Farmland Preservation Program and Oregon's Land Conservation and Development Commission are described.

502. Iowa State University, Center for Agricultural and Economic Adjustment. *Labor Mobility and Population in Agriculture*. Ames, Iowa: Iowa State University Press, 1961. 231 pp.

Collects papers presented at a conference called to analyze the problem of labor supply in, and its transfer from, the agricultural industry.

Contains items 464, 530, 533, 544, 546.

503. Jacobs, James J., Edward B. Bradley, and Andrew Vanvig. *Coal-Energy Development and Agriculture in Northeast Wyoming's Powder River Basin*. RJ-178. Laramie, Wyoming: Agricultural Experiment Station, University of Wyoming, Division of Agricultural Economics, 1982. 77 pp.

Determines the nature and magnitude of coal-mineral and surface-land transactions that have occurred between agricultural operators and coal-energy companies; estimates the benefits and costs of coal mine land reclamation; identifies the potential impact of coal mines on surrounding groundwater aquifers; estimates the cost of increasing the supply of water to anticipated water demand points in the region; and estimates the impact of coal-energy development on agricultural operators.

504. Jolliffe, William.   "Farming in the Rural Urban Fringe in Britain." *The Place of Part-time Farming in Rural and Regional Development* (item 488), pp. 35-41.

Discusses the hazards of farming the rural-urban fringe, the legal constraints, and the visual impact of farming practices on the landscape. Four broad groups are discussed: those who depend on farming for their livelihood, those with supplementary off-farm income, those who hobby farm, and those who have chosen farming as a simple way of life.

505. Jolly, R. W., and D. G. Doye. *Farm Income and the Financial Condition of United States Agriculture*. University of Missouri, Center for National Food and Agricultural Policy, Columbia, Missouri, and Iowa State University, Center for Trade and Agricultural Policy, Ames, Iowa, 1985. 42 pp.

Examines financial stress in agriculture from various viewpoints: origins and issues, current conditions, and policy implications. A conceptual model is proposed to examine the impact of changing economic conditions or government policies on farm income and debt conditions as well as on financial restructuring requirements.

506. Jones, Calvin, and Rachel A. Rosenfeld. *American Farm Women: Findings from a National Survey*. NORC Report No. 130. Chicago, Illinois: National Opinion Research Center, 1981. 238 pp. plus appendixes.

Summarizes findings of a nationwide telephone survey of 2,509 farm women and 569 men conducted during the summer of 1980. Information obtained related to farm women's involvement in the work and management of the farm operation, memberships in farm and community organizations, and participation in the off-farm labor force.

507. Jones, Lonnie L., ed. *Community Development Research in the Great Plains: Abstracts and Major Findings of Research of the NC-102 Regional Project*. GPAC Publ. No. 83. College Station, Texas: Agricultural Experiment Station, Texas A&M University, no date. 58 pp.

Evaluates the effectiveness and costs of providing selected services and facilities in the Great Plains; relates employment opportunities in rural areas of the Great Plains to the labor force; and evaluates alternative institutional arrangements in the economic development of rural communities in the region.

508. Joyce, Lynda M., and Samuel M. Leadley. *An Assessment of Research Needs of Women in the Rural United States: Literature Review and Annotated Bibliography*. University Park, Pennsylvania: Pennsylvania State University, Department of Agricultural Economics, 1977. 116 pp.

Chronologically examines research literature concerning women in rural areas by tracing the development of the research, analyzing the kinds of research undertaken, examining problems and solutions identified in research, looking at how research has been affected by events, and evaluating how research has affected women and women's needs and issues.

509. Kaldor, Donald R., and William M. Edwards. *Occupational Adjustment of Iowa Farmers Who Quit Farming.* Special Rpt. No. 75. Ames, Iowa: Iowa Agricultural Experiment Station, 1975. 46 pp.

Reports the findings from a study of occupational adjustment by Iowa farm operators. Data for the study were obtained by personal interview from a statewide sample of farmers who quit farming and took nonfarm jobs during 1958-61.

510. Khan, Anwar S. *An Economic Analysis of Family Farms in North Carolina: Can They Survive?* Res. Bull. T-132. Greensboro, North Carolina: North Carolina Agricultural and Technical State University, 1985. 89 pp.

Assesses the present condition of small, family, and large farms in North Carolina and attempts to determine the future direction of these farms. The specific objectives are to analyze problems with respect to (1) tenure, types of farm enterprises, and management skills as reflected in farm practices; (2) the relative importance of farm and nonfarm income as it relates to total family income; (3) the attitude of small, family, and large farmers toward their current and future operation; (4) the attitude of county Extension chairmen toward small, family, and large farm operations; (5) a comparison of the three farm sizes in regard to the above objectives; and (6) conditions which place family farmers at a disadvantage in North Carolina's agriculture.

511. Khan, Anwar S. *The Future of Farms in North Carolina As Perceived by County Extension Chairmen.* Res. Bull. Series, Vol. 73, No. 5. Greensboro, North Carolina: North Carolina Agricultural and Technical State University, 1983. 33 pp.

Predicts the future of family farms as perceived by county chairmen of the North Carolina Agricultural

Extension Service. Specifically, farm characteristics according to size, production level, number of enterprises, capital investment, and a host of other relevant factors are analyzed. Secondly, the impact of removal of tobacco quotas, rising cost of energy, and credit on family farms is examined. Thirdly, the role of agricultural extension in meeting the traditional as well as newly created needs of farm operators is assessed separately in the Mountain, Piedmont, and Coastal regions of the state.

512. Khan, Anwar Saeed. *North Carolina Farm Operator Perspectives on Agriculture*. Bull. T-131. Greensboro, North Carolina: North Carolina Agricultural and Technical State University, 1985. 14 pp.

Examines North Carolina farmers' perception of selected agricultural structure issues, their commitment to farming, their perception of farm problems and the agricultural entry process, their long-range plans concerning their farm operations, their familiarity with the Extension Service, and their expectations concerning agricultural land loss.

513. Kopp, Rod. *The Farm Structure Project: Strengthening the Family Farm*. Minneapolis: Minnesota Project, 1980. 107 pp.

Presents a history of American farm policy, then focuses on policy strategies suggested by Minnesota farmers. Issues include farm programs and prices, credit, transportation, conservation, farmland preservation, alternative energy sources, taxes, commodity marketing, corporate farming, and foreign investment.

514. Korsching, Peter F., and Judith Gildner, eds. *Interdependencies of Agriculture and Rural Communities in the Twenty-first Century: The North Central Region*. Ames, Iowa: Iowa State University, North Central Regional Center for Rural Development, 1986. 230 pp.

Collects papers on the nature of changes occurring in agriculture and rural communities. Two major questions were addressed at the conference: What is the role of the agricultural sector in a program of rural development? How can rural development programs improve both agricultural and nonagricultural sectors of rural America?

Contains items 35, 79, 103, 468, 497, 498, 499, 516, 539, 543.

515. Leholm, Arlen G., F. Larry Leistritz, Brenda L. Ekstrom, and Harvey G. Vreugdenhil. *Selected Financial and Other Socioeconomic Characteristics of North Dakota Farm and Ranch Operators.* Agr. Econ. Rpt. No. 199. Fargo: North Dakota Agricultural Experiment Station, 1985. 56 pp.

Presents the results of a 1985 random telephone survey of 933 North Dakota farmers. Specific characteristics examined include: (1) demographic characteristics, such as age, marital status, education, and previous migration patterns; (2) employment history and vocational skills and preferences; (3) participation in community organizations and activities; (4) marketing and trading patterns; (5) farm characteristics, such as acreage operated, principal enterprises, and type of business organization; and (6) financial characteristics, such as levels of assets, debt, and income and sources of credit.

516. Leistritz, F. Larry, Donald E. Albrecht, Arlen G. Leholm, and Steve H. Murdock. "Impact of Agricultural Development on Socioeconomic Change in Rural Areas." *Interdependencies of Agriculture and Rural Communities in the Twenty-first Century: The North Central Region* (item 514), pp. 109-37.

Reviews the trends in agriculture in the North Central region and the outlook for development. The authors then discuss the effects of agricultural development on economic, demographic, and social conditions in rural communities.

517. Leistritz, F. Larry, Harvey G. Vreugdenhil, Brenda L. Ekstrom, and Arlen G. Leholm. *Off-Farm Income and Employment of North Dakota Farm Families.* Agr. Econ. Misc. Rpt. No. 88. Fargo: North Dakota Agricultural Experiment Station, 1985. 48 pp.

Examines the role and significance of off-farm income and employment for North Dakota farm and ranch families. Specific objectives were to estimate the magnitude and major sources of off-farm income for North Dakota farm and ranch families; evaluate the significance of off-farm income for different farm types and for different regions of the state; and determine the farm, household, and personal characteristics that are influential in determining whether farm operators and/or their spouses work off the farm.

518. Lines, Allan E., and Robert Pelly. *1985 Ohio Farm Finance Survey Results.* ESO1214. Columbus, Ohio: Ohio State University, Department of Agricultural Economics, 1985. 48 pp.

Summarizes findings of a 1985 survey of over 900 Ohio farmers conducted by the Statistical Reporting Service. Characteristics reported include operator age and education, farm size and type, gross sales, off-farm income, debt, assets, and debt-to-asset ratio.

519. Loomis, Ralph A. *A Profile of Part-time Farming in the United States.* Agr. Econ. Rpt. 15. East Lansing, Michigan: Michigan State University, Department of Agricultural Economics, 1965. 19 pp.

Gives a brief historical overview of part-time farming and discusses the extent and characteristics of multiple jobholding farmers in the United States as a whole and for specific geographic areas.

520. Loomis, Ralph A. *Working in Two Worlds--Farm and Factory.* Res. Rpt. 32. East Lansing, Michigan: Michigan State University Agricultural Experiment Station, 1965. 12 pp.

Aimed (1) to determine differences in personal characteristics and preferences of multiple jobholding farmers and full-time operators with low farm income; (2) to learn how farmers obtain nonfarm employment, evaluate dual jobholding, and hold attitudes toward occupational preferences, labor unions, and retraining opportunities; and (3) to identify factors of occupational mobility and relate those to income and non-income preferences. Data were from interviews with eighty-nine multiple jobholders and sixty-five full-time operators with low farm income in Kalamazoo and Muskegon counties, Michigan.

521. Mayer, Leo V. "Delineation of Iowa Communities with
      Major Economic Attachment to Agriculture." *Papers of
      the Rural Community Development Seminar: Focus on
      Iowa.* Rural Development Special Series. Ames, Iowa:
      Iowa State University, Center for Agricultural and
      Rural Development, 1972. Section E. 15 pp.

      Discusses the interrelationships between agriculture
      and rural communities by addressing the following
      questions: Where do money flows originate in rural
      towns? Why have these flows changed over time? How
      dependent are different-sized towns on the agricultural
      sector today?

522. Meyer, Neil L., and Richard L. Gardner. *The Financial
      Condition of Idaho Farmers: Signs of Stress in 1985.*
      Bull. No. 646. Boise, Idaho: State of Idaho, Office
      of the Governor, 1985. 16 pp.

      Presents the results of a 1985 random survey of 1,673
      Idaho farmers and ranchers. Survey questions focused
      on demographic, financial, policy, and farm
      information.

523. Michaels, Gregory H., and Gerald Marousek. *Economic
      Impact of Farm Size Alternatives on Rural
      Communities.* Bull. No. 582. Moscow, Idaho: Agri-
      cultural Experiment Station, University of Idaho, May
      1978. 29 pp.

      Seeks to derive empirical measures of the relative
      economic importance of small and large farms, and to
      estimate the income, output, and employment effects of
      farm size alternatives on the rural community. The
      area studied is southern Idaho.

524. Missouri Department of Agriculture (Crop Reporting
      Service), and the University of Missouri-Columbia,
      Department of Agricultural Economics. *Missouri:
      Agricultural Finance Survey.* Columbia, Missouri,
      February 1986. 4 pp.

      Presents results of the January 1986 farm finance
      survey of approximately 2,000 Missouri farmers. Of the
      nine midwestern states conducting similar surveys
      (Illinois, Iowa, Kansas, Michigan, Missouri, Nebraska,
      North Dakota, Ohio, and Wisconsin) Missouri has the
      second lowest average debt-to-asset ratio and the

highest percentage of farmers with debt ratios under 0.40.

525. Molnar, Joseph J. *Alabama Farm Operator Perspectives on a Changing Structure of Agriculture.* Bull. 535. Auburn, Alabama: Alabama Agricultural Experiment Station, 1982. 30 pp.

Examines selected issues and trends in the structure of agriculture from the perspective of the Alabama farmer. The report is addressed to farmers, extension personnel, and others in the agricultural community concerned with the future of farming in Alabama. The results provide a statistical profile of Alabama farm operators' opinions which may be used to anticipate policy preferences and concerns for the future.

526. Murdock, Steve H., Rita R. Hamm, Don E. Albrecht, John K. Thomas, and Janelle Johnson. *The Farm Crisis in Texas: An Examination of the Characteristics of Farmers and Ranchers Under Financial Stress in Texas.* Dept. Tech. Rpt. No. 85-2. College Station, Texas: Texas Agricultural Experiment Station, Department of Rural Sociology, 1985. 186 pp.

Provides information on the characteristics of 1,020 Texas farm and ranch operators who are undergoing different levels of financial stress. Specific objectives of the survey were (1) to examine the severity of the farm crisis among farmers and ranchers in different regions of the state and (2) to examine the characteristics of those farm and ranch operators who are most and least affected by the farm financial crisis.

527. Nobe, Kenneth C., Jerry E. Fruin, Thomas A. Miller, Melvin D. Skold, and Warren L. Trock. *The Agricultural Crisis In Colorado: Causes, Future Prospects, and State-Level Response Options.* ANRE Res. Rpt. AR:86-1. Fort Collins, Colorado: Colorado State University, 1986. 108 pp.

Examines causes of economic stress in the agricultural sector in the mid-1980s; assesses future prospects for agriculture in Colorado and the United States; evaluates several state programs for financial assistance to farmers; and suggests priorities for allocating resources at the federal, state, and university levels.

528. Otto, Daniel. *Analysis of Farmer's Leaving Agriculture for Financial Reasons: Summary of Survey Results from 1984.* Ames: Iowa State University, Cooperative Extension Service, June 1985. 15 pp.

   Presents information from a survey representing 482 Iowa farmers who left agriculture for financial reasons. Included in the analysis is information on demographic characteristics, farm type, method of exiting, causes of becoming overleveraged, residential status, disposition of land, employment status of husband and spouse, and number of years in farming.

529. Ottoson, Howard W., Eleanor M. Birch, Philip A. Henderson, and A. H. Anderson. *Land and People in the Northern Plains Transition Area.* Lincoln, Nebraska: University of Nebraska Press, 1966. 362 pp.

   Focuses on the region of physical and economic transition between the more intensive corn-belt type of agriculture in the eastern fringe of the Great Plains and the wheat or ranching regions of the High Plains. Part I is a historical analysis of the factors which have contributed to the transition area. Part II focuses on central Nebraska--farm size, efficiency, income, farm finance, and capital accumulation. Also considered are population shifts in the transition area, public services, and the situation of the small town. Part III is a discussion of the future of rural communities in the Northern Plains and an examination of social and economic alternatives which may affect readjustment and the rate of economic development.

530. Parnes, Herbert. "Improving Functioning of Nonfarm Labor Market as Related to Mobility Needs." *Labor Mobility and Population in Agriculture* (item 502), pp. 220-26.

   Advances the thesis that the problem of encouraging transfers from the farm to the nonfarm labor force is conceptually identical with the problem of minimizing structural unemployment generally.

531. Perkins, Brian B. *Multiple Jobholding Among Farm Operators: A Study of Agricultural Adjustment in Ontario.* Guelph, Ontario: University of Guelph, School of Agricultural Economics, 1972. 56 pp.

Examines the incidence of multiple jobholding among farm operators in Ontario. One hundred farmers in Grey County were surveyed. The report discusses the nature of nonfarm employment, factors contributing to multiple jobholding, financial benefits of off-farm work, and multiple jobholding as a form of economic adjustment or transition into other employment.

532. Powers, Ronald C., and Daryl J. Hobbs. "Changing Relationships Between Farm and Community." *The Farm and Food System in Transition: Emerging Policy Issues.* FS46. East Lansing, Michigan: Michigan State University, Cooperative Extension Service, 1985. 6 pp.

Examines changes in relationships between agriculture and rural communities that have occurred since 1950 and suggests the implications of the changing relationship with respect to policy issues related to agriculture and rural development. The authors indicate that agriculture has become a less important part of the economic base of many communities and that increasingly the structure of farming is affected by the nature of the rest of the area economy.

533. Raup, Philip M. "Economic Aspects of Population Decline in Rural Communities." *Labor Mobility and Population in Agriculture* (item 502), pp. 95-106.

Delineates the changes in rural communities brought about by the truck transport revolution and examines the nature of the changing configuration of rural villages in American agriculture, the reasons that have brought it about, and some of the private and public costs associated with the change.

534. Rogers, Jack E. *Part-time Farming in New York State, 1930-1969: The Effects of Development of Agricultural Mechanization, Employment Opportunities, and Transportation.* Ithaca, New York: Cornell University, 1981. 176 pp.

Explores the history of part-time farming then examines the current growth in the percentage of farmers engaged in part-time farming within the context of a simple modernization hypothesis that part-time farming is stimulated by the development and availability of labor-saving agricultural machinery, off-farm employment, and transport access to that employment.

535. Ruttan, Vernon W. *Technical Change and Innovation in Agriculture*. Discussion Paper 26. Minneapolis: University of Minnesota, Strategic Management Research Center, 1985. 52 pp.

Refers to the evidence on productivity growth and on the returns to agricultural research, reviews the changing role of the public and private sector in agricultural research, discusses the dominant role of factor prices in directing productivity growth, and suggests some implications of the agricultural experience.

536. Salant, Priscilla, and William Saupe. "Farm Household Viability: Policy Implications from the Wisconsin Family Farm Survey." *Economic Issues* 97(April 1986). 4 pp. Available from the University of Wisconsin-Madison, Department of Agricultural Economics.

Discusses implications of policies specifically targeted at farm families who are in the most severe financial trouble. The discussion is organized by dairy and nondairy farmers and by part-time and full-time farmers.

See also item 537.

537. Salant, Priscilla, William Saupe, and John Belknap. *Highlights of the 1983 Wisconsin Family Farm Survey*. R3294. Madison, Wisconsin: University of Wisconsin-Madison, 1984. 7 pp.

Summarizes results of on-farm surveys of 529 family farm operators in southwestern Wisconsin. Results are organized by farm business size, financial circumstances, employment, and sources of income. The survey is the second phase of a family farm research program.

See also item 536.

538. Sanford, Scott, Luther Tweeten, Cheryl Rogers, and Irving Russell. *Origins, Current Situation and Future Plans of Farmers in East Central Oklahoma*.

Res. Rpt. P-861. Stillwater, Oklahoma: Oklahoma State University, Agricultural Experiment Station in cooperation with Langston University, Agricultural Research Center, Langston, Oklahoma, November 1984. 30 pp.

Analyzes differences in the organizational structure, enterprise mix, resource availability, and future plans of farm operators by status (part-time, full-time, and aged operators) and by size as measured by sales (receipts). The study also examines the entry, current situation, and future plans of minorities and of other operators classified by total family income.

539. Sauer, Richard J. "Agriculture and the Rural Community: Opportunities and Challenges for Rural Development." *Interdependencies of Agriculture and Rural Communities in the Twenty-first Century: The North Central Region* (item 514), pp. 1-11.

Identifies and explores the opportunities and challenges for rural development projects, activities, and programs for the following groups: (1) research and extension faculty from land-grant universities; (2) state, regional, and national administrators from USDA; and (3) non-land-grant representatives, such as economic and rural development groups and agencies and commodity organizations.

540. Saupe, William E., and Bruce Weber. *Rural Family Income in Wisconsin.* Res. Rpt. R2634. Madison, Wisconsin: University of Wisconsin, College of Agricultural and Life Sciences, Research Division, 1974. 43 pp.

Describes the income characteristics of 1,021 rural farm and nonfarm residents of Wisconsin and relates income to a measure of family well-being.

541. Scott, John T., Jr. *The Financial Condition of Farmers in Illinois.* AE-4603. Urbana-Champaign, Illinois: University of Illinois, 1985. 26 pp.

Uses data drawn from the Farm Bureau Farm Management record system to describe the financial position of Illinois farmers. Effects of declining farm income and asset values on other sectors are briefly discussed.

542. Scott, John T., Jr., and James D. Johnson. *The Effect
      of Town Size and Location on Retail Sales.* Ames,
      Iowa: North Central Regional Center for Rural
      Development, 1976. 134 pp.

      Attempts (1) to determine the range of retail goods
      provided by different sizes of urban places in two
      predominantly different rural states, (2) to investi-
      gate the relationship of distance to larger urban
      places on the retail offerings of small towns, and (3)
      to estimate the effects of location (i.e., nearness)
      and town size on community viability as reflected in
      retail sales. Data were drawn from the Census of
      Retail Trade for the years 1954, 1958, 1963, and 1967
      for all Iowa and Illinois communities with populations
      exceeding 2,500. Correlation and regression analyses
      were used to analyze trade patterns.

543. Shaffer, Ron, Priscilla Salant, and William Saupe.
      "Rural Economies and Farming: A Synergistic Link."
      *Interdependencies of Agriculture and Rural Communi-
      ties in the Twenty-first Century: The North Central
      Region* (item 514), pp. 55-72.

      Briefly reviews three theoretical constructs
      (welfare, export base, and central place theories)
      explaining the interaction between farming and rural
      communities. Specific linkages are then explored
      including nonfarm jobs and income, availability of
      consumer goods, and the link between export and
      nonexport activities.

544. Shannon, Lyle W. "Occupational and Residential Adjust-
      ment of Rural Migrants." *Labor Mobility and Popula-
      tion in Agriculture* (item 502), pp. 122-50.

      Examines the adjustment process of rural migrants to
      urban areas. Results indicate that status was improved
      through migration to urban areas and integration into
      the urban-industrial society.

545. Sonka, Steven T., and Earl O. Heady. *Income and Struc-
      ture of American Agriculture Under Future Alterna-
      tives of Farm Size, Policies and Exports.* CARD
      Report 53. Ames, Iowa: Center for Agricultural and
      Rural Development, 1975. 109 pp.

Examines policy alternatives and various outcomes for agriculture if the industry took on various structures in size and technology, and measures, in relation to policies and farm sizes that might prevail in the future, the effects of farm commodity prices, returns in the farm sector, employment and input requirements of agriculture, capital needs of the industry, consumer food costs, and generation of employment and income in the rural nonfarm sector.

546. Taves, Marvin J. "Consequences of Population Loss in Rural Communities." *Labor Mobility and Population in Agriculture* (item 502), pp. 107-21.

Examines the effects of outmigration on rural communities first in a historical context and then by type of community resident (youth, productive outmigrant aged twenty-five to sixty, and older outmigrant).

547. Tinley, H. *The Changing Village: A Study of Villages in Hampshire, Wiltshire, and Dorset.* Stoneleigh, Kenilworth, Warwickshire, United Kingdom: Arthur Rank Centre, National Agricultural Centre, 1982. 38 pp.

Provides an overview of the villages and rural areas in England, discusses the relationship of agriculture and rural communities, and describes the characteristics of the survey area. Altogether, six communities were studied in terms of community viability and special requirements of the farming population.

548. University of California. *Technological Change, Farm Mechanization and Agricultural Employment.* Berkeley, California: University of California, Division of Agricultural Sciences, 1978. 243 pp.

Collects six papers prepared for a 1978 workshop concerned with the issues surrounding the use of labor on farms. Specific questions addressed were as follows: What do we know about employment, wage rates, fringe benefits, and labor displacement by machines? What are the implications of continuing technical advance and mechanization for farm operators, workers, and consumers? What might society accomplish with various programs in cushioning the negative impacts on displaced human beings?

549. University of Minnesota. *The Financial Crisis in Minnesota's Agricultural Industry.* St. Paul: University of Minnesota, Institute of Agriculture, Forestry, and Home Economics, 1985. 8 pp.

Presents a comprehensive statement regarding the financial crisis in Minnesota agriculture and its impact on the state's economy, rural communities, and family stress.

550. University of Missouri-Columbia. *Can the Family Farm Survive?* Special Rpt. 219. Report of a Seminar Sponsored by M. G. and Johnnye D. Perry Foundation and the University of Missouri, 9-10 November 1978 at Columbia, Missouri. Columbia, Missouri: University of Missouri, 1978. 77 pp.

Collects papers addressing such topics as technology, agricultural structure, capital, taxes, environment, small farmers, and trends in selected developed countries.

Contains item 496.

551. University of Missouri-Columbia. *Farm and Rural Life Poll.* Columbia, Missouri: University of Missouri, Department of Rural Sociology, 1985. 22 pp.

Summarizes information from the 1985 survey of over 2,100 farm operators in Missouri on the following topics: the current status of the farm family; life in farm communities and rural areas; farm theft and vandalism; farmers' views about price supports, production controls, and other farm-related policies; farmers' concerns about debt; and farmers' perspectives on the future.

552. University of Missouri-Columbia. *Rural Missouri 1995: Challenges and Issues.* Columbia: University of Missouri, Department of Agricultural Economics, 1985. 24 pp.

Summarizes interviews with governmental leaders, organization executives, and university administrators and researchers regarding the major issues and concerns of agriculture and rural communities. Five task forces focused on the following issues: economic base, resource base, rural infrastructure, community, and technology. Also presented are results of a perceptions questionnaire administered to citizens attending one of nineteen meetings around the state.

553. Voelker, Stanley W., Delmer L. Helgeson, and Harvey G. Vreugdenhil. *A Functional Classification of Agricultural Trade Centers in North Dakota.* Agr. Econ. Rpt. No. 125. Fargo, North Dakota: North Dakota Agricultural Experiment Station, North Dakota State University, Department of Agricultural Economics in cooperation with the USDA, Economics, Statistics, and Cooperatives Services, 1978. 51 pp.

Develops a functional agricultural trade center classification scheme based upon retail and professional services available to each center. The study focused on 135 North Dakota cities that had a 1970 population ranging between 300 and 3,000. Nearly all were primarily or entirely agriculturally dependent communities.

554. Walden, M. L. *Lessons Farmers Can Learn From Economic Hard Times.* AG-294. Raleigh, North Carolina: North Carolina State University, 1982. 13 pp.

Discusses three economic lessons: (1) interest rates and inflation, (2) recession, and (3) market-specific factors affecting agriculture.

555. Wallace, L. Tim, and David Strong. *Selected Economic Estimates of the Impact of Restricting Irrigation Inflows to Agricultural Lands in the Westlands Water District of California.* Berkeley, California: University of California, Cooperative Extension, April 1985. 30 pp.

Estimates the direct and indirect economic impacts of a reduction in irrigation water delivered to a specific acreage on the West Side of the San Joaquin Valley in Fresno County. These inpacts may occur in gross private sector economic activity and in the returns to and costs of local government.

556. Wardle, Christopher, and Richard N. Boisvert. *Farm and Non-Farm Alternatives For Limited Resource Dairy Farmers in Central New York.* AE Res. 74-6. Ithaca, New York: Cornell Agricultural Experiment Station, 1974. 56 pp.

Attempts to identify the income problems faced by
small farmers and to determine the causes of those
problems. Both farm and nonfarm alternatives that
might increase the income of small farms were explored,
and recommendations for educational programs which will
assist farmers in taking full advantage of these alternatives are made. A survey of 81 farms conducted in
1973 provided data for the analysis.

557. Watt, David L., James A. Larson, Glenn D. Pederson, and
     Brenda L. Ekstrom. *The Financial Status of North
     Dakota Farmers and Ranchers: January 1, 1985, Survey
     Results.* Agr. Econ. Rpt. 207. Fargo, North Dakota:
     North Dakota State University, Department of Agricul-
     tural Economics, 1986. 55 pp.

     Presents a detailed analysis of data obtained from a
     1985 survey of over 1,300 North Dakota farmers and
     ranchers. Major topics discussed are real and nonreal
     estate delinquency and the financial position by debt-
     to-asset ratio categories for various financial and
     demographic characteristics.

558. Williams, Anne S., and Allen C. Bjergo. *Strategies for
     Successful Small Scale Farming: A Profile of 43
     Montana Farm Families.* Bull. 742. Bozeman, Montana:
     Montana Agricultural Experiment Station, 1982. 13
     pp.

     Documents the experiences of forty-three Montana
     families with small-scale farms for the purpose of
     identifying alternative management strategies that
     small-scale operators elsewhere may wish to consider.
     In addition, other management strategies with potential
     application to small-scale agriculture are discussed.

Dissertations and
Unpublished Papers

Dissertations and Unpublished Papers

559. Barlett, Peggy F. "'The Disappearing Middle' and Other Myths of the Changing Structure of Agriculture." Paper presented at the Conference on Agricultural Change: Consequences for Southern Farms and Rural Communities, 9-11 October 1985 at Atlanta, Georgia. Available from the author at Emory University, Department of Anthropology, Atlanta, Georgia 30322. 25 pp.

Discusses the fallacies of four popular assertions being made about the current situation and future of U.S. agriculture: (1) that part-time farmers have taken jobs to "save the family farm," (2) that full-time family farms are a "disappearing middle" between the part-time farms and the large commercial farms, (3) that farming conditions are so difficult that barriers to entry for young farmers are nearly insurmountable, and (4) that large-scale superfarms are the way of the future.

560. Barlett, Peggy F. "Part-time Farming: Saving the Farm or Saving the Lifestyle." Available from the author at the Department of Anthropology, Emory University, Atlanta, Georgia 30322. January 1986. 42 pp.

Presents results of an in-depth study of a Georgia county characterized by row-crop and livestock operations and concludes that most part-time farmers are not "trying to save the family farm" but instead have rejected full-time farming in favor of a commitment to off-farm work early in life. Later, these well-educated and comfortably off families added a farm for a combination of economic and lifestyle benefits. A minority of part-time farmers have recently been forced out of full-time farming, and a third group of investors reveals the diversity of this sector.

561. Breimyer, Harold F. "Government, Agriculture, and the Rural Community in the 1980s." Paper prepared for a

panel discussion, "Revival for Survival in Rural
Areas," at the annual meeting of the National Rural
Electric Cooperative Association, 8 February 1982 at
Atlanta, Georgia. Available from the author as Paper
No. 1982-10 of the University of Missouri-Columbia,
Department of Agricultural Economics, Columbia,
Missouri 65201. 4 pp.

Discusses the responsiblity of the government to
provide a leadership role for rural areas in the face
of a declining agricultural economy.

562. Breimyer, Harold F. "Rural America: The Present
Crisis." Opening address given at the Workshop on
Rural Concerns, Rural Life Committee, Mt. St.
Scholastica Convent, 28 June 1982 at Atchinson,
Kansas. Available from the author at the University
of Missouri, Department of Agricultural Economics,
Columbia, Missouri 65201. 8 pp.

Remarks on disparities existing within agriculture
and rural America (1) through a review of the heritage
of the United States and the place of agriculture and
rural communities in it and (2) an account of economic
policies of the last decade and their consequences for
both rural and urban Americans.

563. Chicoine, David L. "Off-Farm Income, Farm Structure,
and Rural Economies: A Policy Perspective." Paper
presented at the Organized Symposium: Policy Issues
on the Role and Development of a National Rural
Development Policy, American Agricultural Economics
Association Meetings, 5-7 August 1984 at Cornell
University, Ithaca, New York. Available from the
author as Rpt. No. 84-E-300 at the Department of
Agricultural Economics, University of Illinois,
Urbana, Illinois 61801. 14 pp.

Concludes that a strong agricultural sector is dependent on a healthy balanced rural economy as a source of
income and economic stability. From a policy perspective, successful public programs to encourage economic
diversification and revitalization in rural areas are
beneficial to the farm sector by providing off-farm
employment opportunities. These opportunities appear
to be to the advantage of not only farmers wishing to
combine farm and nonfarm careers but also to farm

spouses interested in supplementing family incomes as well as pursuing their own professional careers.

564. Drielsma, Johannes Hendrik. "The Influence of Forest-Based Industries on Rural Communities." Ph.D. Dissertation. New Haven, Connecticut: Yale University, 1984. 300 pp.

Explores the interrelationships between forestry, forest-based industries, and the stability and quality of life in forestry-dependent communities. Results indicate that forestry communities are among the least prosperous of all rural communities and that they are dominated by nonlocal forces.

565. Fitzsimmons, Margaret Irene. "Consequences of Agricultural Industrialization: Environmental and Social Change in the Salinas Valley, California 1945-1978." Ph.D. Dissertation. Los Angeles: University of California, 1983. 400 pp.

Analyzes the sources of change in the structure of capital in Salinas Valley agriculture and the consequences of such change for labor and for the natural environment.

566. Flora, Jan L. "The Farm Crisis and Decatur County." Draft report available from the author at Kansas State University, Department of Sociology, Anthropology, and Social Work, Manhattan, Kansas 66506. September 1985. 102 pp.

Studies a dryland wheat-livestock county in northwestern Kansas to assess the extent to which farming is the driving force in the economy and social life of the county and its county seat versus the extent to which the service economy and transfer payments have come to play a major role.

567. Flora, Jan L., and Cornelia Butler Flora. "Emerging Agricultural Technologies, Farm Size, Public Policy, and Rural Communities: The Great Plains and the West." Contribution 85-536-B. Report submitted to the Office of Technological Assessment. Available from the authors at the Agricultural Experiment Station, Department of Sociology, Anthropology, and Social Work, Manhattan, Kansas 66502. 1985. 36 pp.

Attempts to determine how changes in the structure of
agriculture (particularly wheat- and livestock-based
farming enterprises) affect the welfare of agricultural
communities in the Great Plains and West of the United
States.

568. Gottfried, Robert Richard. "The Impact of Recreation
Communities on Land Prices in the Local Community:
The Case of Beech Mountain." Ph.D. Dissertation.
Chapel Hill, North Carolina: University of North
Carolina, 1981. 188 pp.

Develops a model of a recreation land market in a
rural area adjacent to a recreation community. The
analysis indicates that the main effect of the Beech
Mountain resort on area land prices may have been to
attract large numbers of outsiders who responded
differentially to economic stimuli and who often paid
higher prices than locals for land.

569. Hass, Jannette Jean. "The Effect of Community Attachment on Purchase Location of Goods and Services Among
Farmers." Master's thesis. Ames, Iowa: Iowa State
University, Department of Sociology and Anthropology,
1983. 51 pp.

Focuses on three counties in eastern Iowa to examine
the effect community attachment has on shopping
patterns among farmers. The value of community attachment as a predictor variable is also examined.

570. Hatle, Harlowe, Timothy Borich, and James R. Stewart.
"Nonfarm Jobs and the Changing Farm." Paper
presented at the Midwest Sociological Society
meetings, 27 March 1986 at Des Moines, Iowa. Available from the senior author at the University of
South Dakota, Vermillion, South Dakota 57069.

Investigates the effect of manufacturing versus
nonmanufacturing jobs on the number of farms in an
area, specifically Iowa.

571. Henry, Mark, Agapi Somwaru, Gerald Schluter, and
William Edmonson. "Some Effects of Farm Size on the
Nonfarm Economy." Available from the senior author
at the Department of Agricultural Economics, Clemson
University, Clemson, South Carolina 29631. 1985. 14
pp.

Considers impacts on nonfarm sectors of the economy
if U.S. agriculture were composed of fewer medium-sized
farms and more large farms. Using input-output
analysis, the authors estimate the change in nonfarm
output that would be required to support a new size
distribution of farms in the U.S.

572. Hitz, Gregory Henry. "Part-time Farming in Grenada:
Factors Affecting Off-farm Work by Small Operators."
Ph.D. Dissertation. College Park, Maryland: Univer-
sity of Maryland, 1984. 208 pp.

Examines a theoretical model explaining allocation of
time by farm operators to on- and off-farm work. The
model attempts to explain participation and hours of
off-farm work among a cross section of farmers in three
rural areas of Grenada, West Indies.

573. Johnson, Randell A. "A Study of Mobility and Career
Patterns of Part-time and Full-time Farmers."
Master's thesis. Madison, Wisconsin: Cooperative
Extension Administration, University of Wisconsin,
1967. 76 pp.

Examines occupational mobility and career patterns of
399 farm operators in relation to farm and nonfarm work
for three time periods—prior to 1957, 1957, and 1964.

See also items 200, 204.

574. Loven, W. Robert. "Rural Communities and Agriculture
Interdependency: Strategic 'Futures'." Paper
presented to the Joint Council on Food and Agricul-
ture Sciences, 2 May 1985 at USDA, Washington, D.C.
Available from the author at the Federal Extension
Service, USDA, Washington, D.C. 29 pp.

Presents a conceptual framework for anticipating
needed actions, events, or conditions that may not be
based on past experiences or current situations and
that relate to the interdependencies of agriculture and
rural communities.

575. Miller, Thomas A., Thomas A. Stucker, Matthew Smith,
Kenneth Krause, and David Harrington. "The Changing
Financial Structure of the U.S. Farm Sector." ANRE
Working Paper WP:85-5. Fort Collins, Colorado:

Colorado State University, Department of Agricultural
and Resource Economics, 1985.   25 pp.

Examines current trends in the financial structure
and organization of the U.S. farm sector and formulates
hypotheses   concerning   future   changes   in   these
dimensions. A point of special interest is the growing
importance of off-farm income to farm families.   In
1983 off-farm income accounted for 72% of the total
income of farm operator families, compared to 64% in
1980, 55% in 1970, and 42% in 1960.

576. Moore, Keith M.   "The Household Labor Allocation of
      Farm-Based Families in Wisconsin."   Ph.D. Disserta-
      tion.   Madison, Wisconsin: University of Wisconsin,
      1984. 409 pp.

Focuses on the determinants and consequences of the
differential   allocation of   labor by members of farm-
based households in the production and   reproduction of
their existence.   Emphasis is placed on the structure
of agriculture and its relationship to broader changes
in the organization of productive activities throughout
the economy.   A sample of Wisconsin farm families
provided the data base for the analysis.

577. Raup, Philip M.   "The Crisis in Agriculture."   Staff
      Paper P85-34.   St. Paul: University of Minnesota,
      Department of Agricultural and Applied Economics,
      1985. 11 pp.

Examines forces which led to the difficult economic
and financial conditions facing American agriculture in
the mid 1980s and assesses the implications of the
financial situation for farmers, agribusiness, and
rural communities.

578. Reif, Linda L.   "Farm Structure, Industry Structure and
      Socioeconomic Conditions: A Longitudinal Study in
      Economy and Society."   Ph.D. Dissertation. Raleigh,
      North Carolina: North Carolina State University,
      Department of Sociology and Anthropology, 1986.

Analyzes the effects of farm and industrial structure
on socioeconomic conditions of a county, the effects of
socioeconomic conditions and industrial structure on
farm structure, and the   effects of farm structure on

industrial structure. Data for almost all 3,037 U.S.
counties for the 1970 and 1980 time periods were used.

579. Rodefeld, Richard Donald. "The Changing Organizational
     and Occupational Structure of Farming and the Impli-
     cations for Farm Work Force Individuals, Families and
     Communities." Ph.D. thesis. Madison, Wisconsin:
     University of Wisconsin, 1974. 698 pp. plus
     appendix.

     Attempts to satisfy the need for more definitive
     information on the causes, effects, and trends in farm
     change generally and on family and corporate farms
     specifically. Interviews were conducted with owner-
     managers, hired managers, and hired workers of family-
     sized and larger-than-family-sized farms in Wisconsin.
     Hypotheses concerning differences among these groups
     with respect to socioeconomic characteristics, family
     structure, and community involvement were tested using
     a variety of statistical techniques.

580. Sexton, Roger Neil. "Determinants of Multiple Job-
     Holding by Farm Operators." Unpublished Ph.D.
     thesis. Raleigh, North Carolina: North Carolina
     State University, Department of Economics and
     Business, 1975. 154 pp.

     Investigates the factors affecting the amount of
     labor time supplied to off-farm work by farm operators.
     A theoretical model of multiple jobholding is first
     developed in order to identify the principal factors
     influencing the secondary labor supply of farm
     operators. Cross-sectional data relating to farm
     operators in the tobacco-producing areas of the south-
     eastern United States and in the mixed farming areas of
     the state of Illinois are then used to develop empir-
     ical estimates of the effects of these different
     variables.

581. Sussman, Jean Cecele. "A Comparison of Part-time and
     Full-time Agricultural Operations in Dodge County,
     Minnesota." Ph.D. Dissertation. St. Paul: Univer-
     sity of Minnesota, Department of Agricultural
     Economics, 1985. 344 pp.

     Examines and discovers three groups of operations
     among part- and full-time farmers in southern

Minnesota: hobby operations, part-time expansion-
oriented operations, and full-time operations.

582. Swanson, Larry Douglas.   "A Study in Socioeconomic
       Development: Changing Farm Structure and Rural
       Community Decline in the Context of the Technological
       Transformation of U.S. Agriculture." Unpublished
       Ph.D. dissertation. Lincoln, Nebraska: University
       of Nebraska, 1980. 319 pp.

       Evaluates the extent to which important elements of
       rural community structure in an agricultural region of
       Nebraska are differentiated according to key components
       of the area's farm structure.   The author argues that
       the viability of rural, agricultural communities is to
       a large degree a function of, or derived from, the
       nature of the area's farm structure.   Data from twenty-
       seven rural, agricultural counties for the period 1940-
       1974 were used in the analysis.   Elements of farm
       structure used in the analysis included (1) number of
       farms, (2) average farm size, (3) percent of farms over
       1,000 acres, (4) operator age distribution, and (5)
       value of farm products sold per farm.   Elements of
       community structure considered in the analysis included
       (1) total population, (2) nonfarm population, (3)
       dependency ratio, (4) school enrollment, (5) civilian
       labor force, (6) number of retail trade establishments,
       and (7) number of service establishments.

Indexes

Author Index

183

Subject Index